Forensic Pathology

Preventing Wrongs

Satish Sekar

With a Foreword by Michael Mansfield QC

THE FITTED-IN PROJECT

"Satish is a man on a mission to unmask science, rather to unmask men and women who cover their prejudice under the cloak of science. His incisive writings leave us pondering: if science is detached and disinterested, could the same be said about scientists? This book exposes abortion of justice. It locates the crime scene where it's least expected — at the court of law.

One of the cases he mentions touches me personally. I know for a fact that the Eikenhof Three are innocent — they always were. APLA claimed responsibility immediately, and the science supported their claim, but still almost 20 years after the three ANC members were freed, the causes of that injustice remain unaddressed. We need a Truth and Justice Commission in South Africa too."

Letlapa Mphahlele[1]

---

1. Letlapa is a former Azanian People's Liberation Army (APLA) commander, and past President of the Pan Africanist Congress of Azania (PAC). He is a former MP in South Africa and remains active fighting for justice. Letlapa is also the author of several books, including **Child Of This Soil — My Life As A Freedom Fighter**. He received a report on the Eikenhof attack from its commander, which the police — Apartheid was dying at the time — had consequently seized. This means the authorities knew that the Eikenhof Three (Siphiwe Bholo, Zipho Gavin and Titi 'Boy' Ndweni) were innocent long before their eventual release.

Forensic Pathology
Preventing Wrongs
Satish Sekar

ISBN 978-0-9527325-2-5 (Paperback)

Cataloguing-In-Publication Data A catalogue record for this book can be obtained from the British Library.

Published 2019 by
The Fitted-In Project Ltd.
6 Cheston Close, Longford, Gloucester, GL2 9FG, United Kingdom.

Email satishcsekar@fittedin.org
Web fittedin.org

Table of Contents

This book is dedicated to a very special person, the late great Bob Woffinden.[1] He was far more than just a superb journalist; he was an exemplary human being and an inspiration to me. He is sorely missed.

1. Bob Woffinden (1948–2018) sadly died on May 1st of a rare form of cancer, mesothelioma, but not before establishing himself as a colossus of journalism. While he will be remembered for his pioneering work in miscarriages of justice—there was hardly any major injustice that he wasn't involved in fighting against—Bob was a gifted music journalist, TV producer and author, and West Bromwich Albion supporter.

When I was getting started—my first case was the Cardiff Five—Bob was always available to help and provide invaluable assistance and advice. As a friend and colleague, I miss him, but value the time we had. He remains one of the great inspirations to me.

Acknowledgements

The Fitted-In Project and the author greatly appreciate the contributions of Professor Dave Barclay, Richard Eikelenboom and Andrew Rennison in particular. Without their assistance and generosity this book could not have been written. We would also like to thank Roger Backhouse QC, Raju Bhatt, Daryl Clemens, Mpagi Edward Edmary, Dave Eyre, Edward Fitzgerald QC, Alex Gibson, Bryan Gibson, Bishop Gregg Greer, Michael Mansfield QC, Rajiv Menon QC, Professor Robert Moles, Letlapa Mphahlele, Ashley Muench, Angela Sayers and Richard Sayers for their encouragement and assistance.

Thanks are also due to Richard Adams, Dev Barrah, Victor Boremann, Liberty Bridge, Duncan Campbell, Sharon Clarke, Bettina Dix, the late Trish Donald, Dr Dennis Eady, Stacy Hough, Stuart Hutton, Dean Jones, Kervin Julien, John Kamara, Ronald Katongole, Traolach Kaye, Dr Sandra Lean, John McManus, Louis Martin, Alun Michael, Derek Miller, Ian Moore, Iain Murray, Alanna Nicholls, Anthony Parris, Michael Parris, Govind Dutt Pullat, Britta Slopianka, Surya Suma Panicker, Dave Tapp, Jennifer Thompson, Carol Toal, Ruwan Uduwerage-Perera, Allan Waltham and Kate Williams.

About the author

Satish Sekar is a freelance journalist and researcher. His work includes for the feature-film *In the Name of the Father*, and TV and radio programmes such as *Panorama, Trial and Error, Law in Action, Today, The Black Bag, Black Ink* and *Channel 4 News*. He has written for the *Guardian, Independent, Daily Telegraph, The Voice* and *Private Eye*. He also covers sport, especially football and cricket, mainly for *EmpowerS Magazine*.

In 1998, his book **Fitted In: The Cardiff 3 and the Lynette White Inquiry** was published by **The Fitted-In Project**, a justice organisation, of which he is the founding director, and now CEO. Shortly after it was published, the case was actively re-opened by a new unit set up to investigate unsolved and unresolved homicides, leading in 2003, to the real killer, Jeffrey Gafoor, pleading guilty to Lynette White's murder—the first time in British history that people originally convicted (or wrongfully accused) were vindicated by the conviction of the person truly guilty of the murder in the DNA age.

A consultant on forensic matters, Satish Sekar has been involved in various high profile issues, including in relation to police reform, police complaints, DNA-testing and related databases. In 2012, **Waterside Press** published his second book **The Cardiff Five: Innocent Beyond Any Doubt**—the second edition of which was released in 2017. **Trials and Tribulations: Innocence Matters?** was released in 2017 by **The Fitted-In Project**.

The author of the Foreword

Michael Mansfield QC was called to the Bar in 1967. He established Tooks Chambers in 1984 and became Queen's Counsel in 1989. Michael has represented defendants in criminal trials, appeals and inquiries in some of the most controversial legal cases the country has seen, particularly where issues of Civil Liberty have arisen.

Foreword by Michael Mansfield QC

"Man prefers to believe what he prefers to be true".

A quotation from the controversial sixteenth century Francis Bacon, the philosopher/scientist not the controversial twentieth century artist. Nonetheless there is, strikingly, a point of parallel meaning within the field of art where it is commonly observed that 'beauty is in the eye of the beholder'.

For over 50 years I have practised within a criminal justice system which has been beset by this insidious and often unconscious force which undermines the search for the truth. It underlies many of the notorious miscarriages of justice. At one end of the spectrum it may be imperceptible, at the other it can be readily identified. In either instance there is a substantial risk to the integrity of both observation and investigation and ultimately the judicial system itself.

There is no clearer example than the case of the Cardiff Five, subsequently Three, about which Satish has written extensively and is featured, amongst other examples, in this book. The whole disgraceful saga of the Cardiff case stems from preconception, bias and ultimately dishonesty. Forensic science had and has the potential to prevent this, to provide a safeguard. In his conclusions Satish sets out how this could and should happen by examining an impressive array of cases. There has never been any other critique so searing, thorough and radical as this. Put shortly he advocates crucial categorical imperatives

(i) independent peer-review;

(ii) meticulous crime-scene preservation, examination, analysis, and reconstruction;

(iii) integrated and collated investigation [to which I would add disclosure, the lack of which continues to be a corrosive malaise within the prosecution service].

Sadly none of this is new. It is a return to first principles espoused by the father of scientific method — Francis Bacon, the philosopher/scientist. He straddled a number of disciplines as well as holding high legal office as Attorney General, Lord Chancellor and the first Queens Counsel appointment (designate to Queen Elizabeth I). He can be credited with pioneering a fresh approach to science and scientific method influenced by the 'empiricist' school of philosophy. At its core lies the need for scrupulous observation followed by a rigorous process of inductive logic. Properly conducted it is the basis for one of the most important fundamental scientific principles — ***inter-verifiability***. This enables another observer/scientist to verify both the observations, the reasoning and the conclusions of another.

Forensic pathology, however, in common with other areas of forensic science, has not always carried this out in practice and has made itself vulnerable to the imperfections of subjective vision.

In relation to pathology there are profession-specific reasons. For many decades it has been relatively small and select, dominated by a few big names. Most are identified in this book. Whilst this environment pertained it has been difficult to obtain alternative views, or to find someone to challenge what was regarded as the accepted wisdom. The limited number of new entrants had invariably been trained by those whose opinions needed to be challenged. This atmosphere was not helped by the reverence shown by the judiciary towards certain luminaries. The culture had become ingrained, inbred and virtually unassailable.

It is in these circumstances that subjective factors can begin to thrive and play a part in the scientific process. Examples of such factors are — a police officer attending the post-mortem who lets slip snippets of background information about the victim, the eye witnesses or defendants if there are any. Equally, a lab liaison report which sets out the police theory about what happened in less subtle terms. Then over time the pathologist may himself have formed views about certain offences, offenders and circumstances or may in any event have innate preconceptions about these aspects.

Despite being discernible and detectable factors, their impact on observation and analysis has not been adequately recognised and assessed until quite recently. 'Cognitive' and 'Confirmation' bias has been copiously researched and subject to blind testing with disturbing results. Confirmation bias is arguably the best known phenomenon in which there is a 'tendency to seek out, select and interpret information in ways that validate one's pre-existing beliefs or expectations' [**Cognitive bias and blindness: a global survey of Forensic Science Examiners** — Kukucka, Kassin, Zapf and Dror: *Journal of Applied Research in Memory and Cognition 2017*]. The authors looked at 400 professional scientists in 21 countries.

Across the whole field of forensic science, including pathology, there has to be a greater awareness of the risks of bias and a paradigm shift towards safeguards. Due to a combination of academic research, together with the effect of notable cases, and the indomitable and tireless work of Satish, change is afoot. Part of that shift involves a recognition that science itself is one thing, scientists quite another. We are not dealing with paper equations. In every exercise there is room for interpretive differences, mistake, oversight, faulty machinery, contaminated samples, and most of all bias.

Introduction

Historic

Misinterpretation, manipulation and/or shoddy practice of forensic sciences still has the power to ruin innocent lives, even in the DNA age. This happens on both sides—the innocent who are wrongly accused and the victims of crime who see the guilty go free. In some cases deaths are ruled homicides when they should not be and in others homicides are wrongly thought to be of natural causes. The distress caused by these errors is palpable and can last for several years—lifetimes even—especially if they are not put right. Nowhere is this clearer than with forensic pathology, as it can and does affect other forensic sciences. This is why it is essential for it to be integrated with investigative policing and other forensic sciences. This has been happening over the last decade, but the negative consequences of previous practice have not been addressed. This is not simply a matter of wrongful accusations and convictions, but homicides that have slipped through the net without being reviewed. This is the first publication in a trilogy about forensic pathology that will address these issues and the consequences of them. **Forensic Pathology—Preventing Wrongs** will detail the historic problems and the solutions that were implemented in the mid-2000s to prevent repetition of errors that had plagued forensic science in the past. The second publication **Forensic Pathology—Righting Wrongs** will highlight some of the wrongs, intentional or otherwise, of the past that forensic pathology contributed to, and the third publication **Forensic Pathology—Next Time the Fire**, will focus on the recent past, including the controversial former Home Office forensic pathologist Dr Michael Heath, who is a very good and recent example of a sad trend that has been unchallenged for decades—over a century. The trail of devastated lives that Heath left in his wake illustrates the need—necessity really—for stringent standards in the regulation and control of the quality of work provided in forensic science. It also illustrates the consequences of the failure to provide an integrated approach between the various forensic science disciplines in case-work and with the police too, through the Senior Investigating Officer (SIO). The classic example of this is Professor Sir Bernard Spilsbury, the man termed by some the 'Father of Forensics'. Spilsbury, more than any other, was responsible for turning forensic pathology from what was seen as the 'beastly profession' into a respectable one, although Spilsbury actually inherited the mantle from the expert forensic pathologist who trained him, Sir William Wilcox. Despite the fame and pre-eminence that this expert won in his lifetime, and to the emerging forensic sciences, Spilsbury and Spilsburyism came at a very high price. Spilsburyism prevented the integration of forensic pathology into police investigative procedures for many years, due to Spilsbury's domination of his profession and the reluctance of forensic pathologists to see themselves as part of an investigative team.

Eminent pathologists such as Francis Camps, Donald Teare and Keith Simpson were the next generation. They were known as the Three Musketeers, but they too were prone to serious error as well — some of which were mind-boggling, such as the failure to realise that rigor mortis was departing rather than beginning. That occurred in the ill-fated Maxwell Confait Inquiry in the 1970s and it was a mistake made by both Teare and Simpson. Very serious mistakes were not confined to Britain. Sometimes it even involved the same expert. Bad as the mistakes made by Teare and Simpson were in the Maxwell Confait Inquiry, they pale in comparison to those made by fellow British forensic scientist, Professor James Cameron in the same case — errors that resulted in a shameful miscarriage of justice.

Jurisdictions

Professor Cameron made very serious mistakes in the Maxwell Confait Inquiry — ones that should have cost him his reputation and at the very least helped to correct another awful miscarriage of justice far earlier than it did. Thousands of miles away in Australia's Northern Territory — Lindy and Michael Chamberlain had cause to rue the day they heard his name. Cameron's opinion that their baby daughter Azaria had been murdered rather than taken by a dingo was based on his examination of ultra-violet photographs. It took more than three decades to put right. Lindy had been convicted of murder and Michael (they subsequently divorced) of being an accessory after the fact a decade after Cameron's deeply flawed pathology had set in motion the unfortunate chain of events that resulted in the wrongful convictions of the Catford Three[1] (Colin Lattimore, Ronald Leighton and Ahmet Salih). In 1986 the chance discovery of Azaria's matinée jacket in an area frequented by dingoes resulted in a successful appeal two years later. Their first appeal had been rejected in 1984. The 'expert' evidence had fallen apart. In 2012 a third inquest resulted in Coroner Elizabeth Morris attributing Azaria's death to being attacked and carried away by a dingo. But Australia was not finished with flawed forensic pathology.

In December 2014 the long-standing case of Henry Keogh hit the headlines again. After two decades the Supreme Court of South Australia quashed Keogh's conviction for the 1994 murder of Anna-Jane Cheney. Keogh's conviction relied on the forensic pathology of Colin Manock[2]—now an experienced pathologist with a heavy case-load of over two and a half autopsies per day for 30 years or so. Manock's evidence came under fire in Keogh's latest appeal. He believed that Cheney had been murdered—drowned in her bath. The method he suggested was similar to that explained by a then plain Bernard Spilsbury when he was making his name in the infamous Brides in the Bath murders—the case which sent George Joseph Smith to the gallows in 1915.[3]

But time would challenge Manock's view. Keogh was convicted in August 1995, mainly due to Manock's opinion that bruises on Cheney's head, back of her neck and lower left leg were consistent with murder. Manock believed that the injuries were consistent with an assailant folding her legs forward to her chest, which forced her head under water and prevented her resisting. The victims of such conduct would quickly lose consciousness and drown, but it could look like an accidental drowning. The problem is that so would an accidental drowning. It was also a circumstantial case that relied on a self-supporting hypothesis in the absence

1. The miscarriage of justice that occurred in the Maxwell Confait Inquiry.
2. For further details on Keogh's case and Dr Manock, see Robert Moles' preface **Dr Manock—The Australian Spilsbury**.
3. For further information on Spilsbury's role in that case and others see **Chapter 3: The Martyr to Spilsburyism** in **Forensic Pathology—Righting Wrongs** (forthcoming).

of conclusive evidence. The forensic science was the cornerstone of the case. It relied on the forensic pathologists Manock and Ross James. After Keogh was convicted an appeal was dismissed along with attempts to re-open the appeal and petitions for mercy too. But Manock later accepted that he had been wrong about a crucial part of his evidence. The jury had been assured that Cheney had been conscious when her head was submerged. Manock recanted that and also withdrew his opinion that all of the injuries had been inflicted within four hours of Cheney's death. The mechanism of death could and should have been challenged too, as there was evidence — never realised, let alone tested at the time — which could and should have demonstrated that the crucial bruising on Cheney's leg had nothing to do with her alleged murder. Unfortunately, the presence of haemosiderin, a product of the healing process of bruising which only becomes present 24 hours after the bruise was suffered, was first mentioned in 2004 by Professor Barrie Vernon-Roberts — a decade late. He recommended that a section of the bruised tissue be tested for it then, but this was not disclosed until 2013. Its significance was obvious, because the discovery of haemosiderin in the bruising to Cheney's leg would have affected the timing of the event that had caused the bruise and that meant that the proof of the mechanism for murder would have been seriously flawed, at best. The testing for haemosiderin was conducted by Professor Anthony Thomas in 2014 and provided confirmation that it was indeed present. This means that the bruising on her leg had actually been there for some time and had not been caused by 'an attack' on her near the time of her death. This undermined the credibility of Manock's evidence given at the trial regarding the mechanism for murder. There was much more affecting the credibility of the pathology evidence, but the appeal court ordered a retrial. On November 13th 2015 Adam Kimber SC (Senior Counsel), South Australia's Director of Public Prosecutions, sensationally told Justice Malcolm Blue at the State's Supreme Court that Keogh would not face a third murder trial over Cheney's death after all. Kimber decided that there was no longer a realistic prospect of conviction because a crucial witness was no longer available to give evidence for health reasons.[4]

---

4. See Robert Moles' website **Networked Knowledge** at http://netk.net.au/KeoghHome.asp for further information on Keogh's case.

Ludicrous Injustice

Manock was far from the only pathologist to exhibit signs of arrogance—hubris even. Kent and England's former opening batsman Bob Woolmer was never one of cricket's greatest players, but unlike many ex-players he made the transition from performing on the field to élite level coaching. He learned his trade in the county cricket circuit in England. Woolmer eventually brought modern methods into coaching and match preparation to the national teams of South Africa and then Pakistan. He worked for Warwickshire and also in developing cricket in smaller nations between his national team jobs. During the 2007 World Cup in the West Indies, Bob Woolmer died suddenly. On March 7th, hours after a humiliating loss to the minnows Ireland that eliminated Pakistan, he died in his hotel room. The rumour-mill rapidly went into overdrive and still has not stopped, but it should never have started. Sadly, the pathologist Ere Seshaiah bears much of the blame for that, but he is not alone. This was a classic case of an utterly botched investigation adding two and two and making a hundred.

The Pakistani team, led by one of the finest batsmen the country produced in recent times, Inzamam ul-Haq, and Vice-captain Mohammad Yousuf (formerly Yousuf Youhana) were treated as suspects in a case that laid the limitations of 'modern' forensic pathology bare. Conspiracy theories spread. Woolmer's death was linked to the match-fixing scandal in South Africa that brought down former captain Hansie Cronje. If not South Africa, then Pakistan would do—after all, that country's cricket had problems with match-fixing and illegal betting and the Pakistani players had easier access to Woolmer. They were playing under his guidance. If they, especially the captain or vice-captain, went to his room, that would hardly be surprising, would it? So they had opportunity and there was no shortage of so-called motive either.

If it was not match-fixing, then religion would do just as well. Ul-Haq, Yousuf and other players were linked to a group named Tableegi Jamaat (TJ), which promoted Islamic beliefs. Woolmer, amongst others, was concerned about their influence in Pakistan's cricket team. Ul-Haq denied applying pressure to other players to join TJ. However, even if Inzamam used his position in Pakistan's team to further the group's views, this was hardly evidence that Woolmer had been murdered. Motive means little or nothing if there was no murder. Nevertheless, the BBC's *Panorama* gained access to the investigation and broadcast a programme that peddled these rumours. Conspicuous by its absence from this programme was an obvious question—one that could have prevented some of Pakistan's best cricketers from being treated like criminals, especially when the evidence not only clears them, but everyone. If Woolmer had been strangled in the bathroom and his body was wedged against that door, how did the murderer(s) get out of the bathroom? It could not be denied as the Scene of Non-Crime photographs proved that Woolmer's body had indeed been slumped against the door of the bathroom. The 'murderer' could not have got out of that bathroom, and that meant there could not have been a murder—it was obvious.

With the world's media in attendance, Ere Seshaiah theatrically declared that Woolmer had been murdered. The cause of death, according to him, was manual strangulation, but there was a problem with his findings—more than one actually. There are reasons for using different techniques for dissecting neck tissue than they use to dissect other tissue. If it is not done using those specific techniques, it will result in marks indicative of strangulation. Despite his certainty on the cause of death, Seshaiah appears to have fallen into this trap, but there is an even more obvious indication that no murder occurred. Woolmer died in the bathroom of his hotel room. His body lay against the door, which opens into the bathroom. How could the alleged murderer have strangled him in the bathroom, left his dead body against the door inside the bathroom and still got out of it and into the main room? Obviously that was impossible, meaning that Woolmer could not have been murdered. But there was no opportunity either. The CCTV had shown nobody leaving or entering Woolmer's hotel suite at the relevant times. All of this meant that all the talk about motives that had taken on a life of its own was nothing more than utterly irresponsible speculation.

The Commissioner of Jamaica's Constabulary Force, Lucius Thomas, responded to further evidence—toxicology reports and the opinions of three pathologists including the esteemed Dr Nat Cary—in June 2007 by declaring that Woolmer had in fact died of natural causes. However,

Seshaiah and others refused to accept it, and they still don't. Despite Thomas' response, the damage had been done by then. Even now, the conspiracy theorists remain unbowed and unashamedly peddle a version of Woolmer's death that cannot be true. It could have and should have been so different. An integrated approach between the forensic pathology and crime-scene analysis—in this case non-crime-scene—should quickly have shown that Bob Woolmer had not been murdered, and that the subsequent treatment of the Pakistani cricketers was outrageous, to put it mildly. Nevertheless, the rumour-mill refused to stop and it included some highly respected people in the sport. South Africa's former captain Clive Rice, and former Australian captain and commentator Ian Chappell did not believe that Woolmer died of natural causes and they still don't. While there is plainly a problem of corruption in cricket, and that may even have provided a motive for murder, the evidence of the hotel room and the botched pathology strongly suggest that Woolmer was not murdered.[5]

Despite the evidence clearly indicating that Woolmer had indeed died of natural causes, the inquest jury would have none of it, reaching a verdict that pleases nobody. The open verdict delivered by that jury in November 2007 flew in the face of the evidence. Tempting as it may have been to buy into the conspiracy theories, it simply was not possible to reconcile the position of the body with murder, given the need for any perpetrator to get out of the bathroom after strangling Woolmer. No perpetrator could have made good her or his escape, and wedged Woolmer's body against the door from the main-room side of the door. And the CCTV evidence only supported that view. Consequently, it was far more likely to have been due to natural causes as that was the only conclusion that could be consistent with the evidence in Woolmer's hotel room, analysis of the scene and also the scientific evidence. Woolmer suffered from both diabetes and heart disease.

Hubris

Seshaiah apparently made an error regarding the dissection of neck tissue that no competent and experienced forensic pathologist should make, but

5. For a fuller examination of this case see **Forensic Pathology—Righting Wrongs**, which is a forthcoming publication by **The Fitted-In Project**.

even in this — the current era — both Michael Heath and Paula Lannas also made the same mistake. Like their predecessors, the late Professors Sir Bernard Spilsbury, Donald Teare and James Cameron, Heath and Lannas betrayed a staggering level of professional arrogance. Heath's opinions that contradicted medical fact and the opinions of colleagues were ignored, as Heath could not contemplate the possibility that he could be wrong. This applied to Lannas and Freddy Patel too. Even basic professional courtesy proved lacking.

As in other jurisdictions, competition between police, crime-scene investigators and specialists in various forensic sciences, especially pathology, existed at that time. Each thought their discipline should have precedence, particularly in the recovery of evidence phase. A good example of this was provided by the internationally renowned DNA expert Richard Eikelenboom. He was integrally involved in obtaining evidence that helped to resolve one of the Netherlands' most notorious miscarriages of justice.[6] "All the problems the National Lab has, the FSS [Forensic Science Service] has before", Eikelenboom said. "So what happens then is I was not at the crime-scene, but I was at the lab, which was quite important as you always have the fight between the biologist and pathologist. There's a lot of fighting going on. The biologist says, 'This is my crime-scene; get out of my crime-scene', and the pathologist says, 'This is my body; get out of my body', so you get all kinds of political stuff that I think in UK was solved ten years before that. In Holland it is more or less getting better now, but at that time we were still fighting over the politics of homicide cases".

In fact, it had not been solved in Britain at that time, but it was about to be.

So competition between the experts in different forensic sciences has occurred and in several jurisdictions, even in the high-profile cases. This competition has caused serious problems. A classic error is placing the corpse of a strangulation victim in a body bag along with other evidence,

6. Eikelenboom helped to develop the protocols which he used to obtain Low Template DNA in the Schiedammer Park Murder — Nienke Kleiss. Kees Borsboom was wrongfully convicted of the rape and murder of Kleiss and attempted murder of Maikel Willebrand. Kleiss was just ten-years-old and Willebrand was eleven when they were viciously attacked by Wik Haalmeijer on June 22nd 2000.

as occurred in the summer of 2000 in the Nienke Kleiss Inquiry in the Netherlands. Eikelenboom explains. "The problem with her DNA [obtaining DNA evidence] was that the front side of her body was completely covered with mucus from the bronchia, because she was strangulated", he said. "You know if you strangle someone you get a lot of fluid from the lungs and that was completely moved in the body-bag".

Such an error — one that should never have occurred in this century — resulted in the contamination of other potential evidence. Also, if the original scene has not been recorded in situ and evidence preserved for recovery, the body and crime-scene cannot tell their story accurately. For example, taping of the body for fibres and hairs must obviously be done at the scene, before the body is moved or examined by a pathologist. If the nature and location of evidence has been interfered with, whether by accident or design, such as occurred in the Dutch case referred to above, the value of that evidence has been compromised. The clock cannot be turned back. This is as true now as it was in Spilsbury's day. It is why validated procedures and safeguards are so important. The aura of an expert witness must never replace or trump validated procedures — well, never again — and that applies to any expert, no matter her or his calibre. Nobody should ever be Spilsburyed again.

However, even in the 21st century, some pathologists were reluctant to concede their primacy at the scene, or that they necessarily should work as part of a team under the direction of the Senior Investigating Officer. Their entire background was rooted in the ethos of the sole practitioner, and the culture of omnipotence. 'What is the difference between God and a pathologist? God doesn't think he is a pathologist'. It was not so much an investigators' joke as a truism. Of course, this causes difficulties in spotting when things have gone wrong, but that was widely recognised by police and forensic scientists, and even by many pathologists. Some lawyers and investigators were aware of it too.

Around 2003 the Association of Chief Police Officers (ACPO) set up a small working group to examine the issues and their report created a new environment for governance of forensic pathology in the UK, and their relationship to SIOs.[7] In summary, each pathologist would now have to work within a group practice of at least three, the members of which would peer-review each other's work and conclusions (a practice which had been for many years mandatory for UK forensic scientists). Their work would also be visible to other accredited forensic pathologists on a closed database, controlled by the Home Office. In signing their new contracts, forensic pathologists would now explicitly agree their role and responsibilities, and that they were part of the investigative team, under the SIO. No question, this was a huge step in the right direction, but what about investigations that were conducted under the previous system? Would the wrongs committed then be redressed and if so, how? Important questions though these are, they are beyond the scope of this publication. They will be addressed in the subsequent publications **Forensic Pathology — Righting Wrongs** and **Forensic Pathology — Next Time the Fire**, which **The Fitted-In Project** plans to publish in 2019 and 2020.

Forensic Pathology — Preventing Wrongs sets out the need for a thorough review of the safeguards provided, as a decade ago the discipline moved out of Spilsbury's shadow and into a new era — one where forensic pathology was finally integrated into investigative needs of modern police investigations. Peer-review is an important part of that process, but how effective has it proved to be? Whether cock up or conspiracy, it appears that the procedures did not work as designed in the Lynette White Inquiry — a case that resulted in one of Britain's most notorious miscarriages of justice. Nevertheless, the process that resulted in the integration of forensic pathology into the requirements of 21st Century policing was long overdue.

---

7. At the same time other initiatives were underway. Ralph Leishman's **Review of Forensic Pathology Services in England and Wales** (2003) is an important work. Following a similar process in 1991 the Home Office accredited forensic pathologists through the Register of Forensic Pathologists. It was maintained by the Home Office Policy Advisory Board for Forensic Pathology, which was later replaced by the Pathology Delivery Board. There are other important works on forensic pathology such as Wasserman's Report and later Peter Hutton's **Review of Forensic Pathology in England and Wales** which was delivered to the Minister of State for Crime Prevention in 2015. The research and reports are plenty and have had an effect on the delivery of forensic pathology and its contribution to criminal justice. It is impossible to detail then competently in this book, but they are certainly relevant contributions. They will be considered in the forthcoming **FIP** publications **Forensic Pathology — Righting Wrongs** and their effect in practice in **Forensic Pathology — Next Time The Fire**.

PROLOGUE BY MPAGI EDWARD EDMARY[8]

It Can't Happen

Justice Defrauded

My story is a strange one—it requires a couple of double-takes—and that's just to believe that it was possible, let alone that it was true. The tale I am about to tell you ought to be too far-fetched for a Hollywood script, but it not only happened, but did so within the last three decades. Miscarriages of justice occur. That is not as unusual as it ought to be. People were convicted of a murder that they did not commit. It's still not as unusual as I'd like, and I hope you too. My story is unusual because not only was I innocent, but everybody was. There was no murder. Again, that is not as unusual as it should be. Experts have made mistakes, even those at the top of their profession such as Spilsbury—you'll read more of him later in this book, but he is long dead. His successors continued and those methods and errors were exported, including sadly to my country, Uganda, albeit in a different time and regime.

Even today, we read the horror stories caused by rank bad forensic pathology—in this day and age—in Australia, Canada and elsewhere too. My story is bizarre because it was not just 'expert error' it was an utterly corrupt system. I said earlier that nobody was guilty of the murder I was convicted of, and this is why. My family and that of alleged victim, William Wandyaka, had an ongoing feud. It was June 1981. I

8. Mpagi was the victim of an outrageous miscarriage of justice in Uganda that claimed the life of his cousin, Fred Masembe. Both were convicted of murder in 1982 and sentenced to death. The miscarriage of justice should have been prevented by forensic pathology. The murder victim was alive and well when Mpagi was exonerated on those grounds in 2000. It was too late for Masembe. Denied the medication he needed to fight malaria, he died on death row in 1985 for a crime that not only he did not commit, but one that nobody did. After his vindication, Mpagi has been a vociferous opponent of the death penalty. In September 2016 he addressed the United Nations General Assembly on that subject. He established a school for orphans and the children of death row inmates in his native Uganda. In October 2018 Bill Pelke and other anti-death penalty activists came to Uganda with the Journey of Hope From Violence to Healing, to support Mpagi's organisation, Ugandans Against the Death Penalty, in its fight against the death penalty as Museveni recently announced that he wanted executions to commence once more in Uganda.

was just 26 years-old when I was arrested and indicted for robbery and murder — Milton Obote was the President at the time. His regime was corrupt and was replaced by that of current President, Yoweri Museveni.

Wandyaka's family held a funeral for him, and demanded justice against me and my cousin, Fred Masembe. On April 29th 1982 we were convicted and sentenced to death. However, there was a problem — an enormous one. The man whom we were convicted of murdering was alive and well. His family bribed a local doctor to falsify a death certificate, coerced people into falsely testifying against us and fabricated evidence. It wasn't until eighteen years later that this was accepted and proved.

After a year on death row we appealed, but the Court of Appeal upheld our sentence. From then on, we knew there was nothing we could do and that we were going to die for a crime that had not occurred. We lived every day knowing that we could be taken without warning and be hanged. Just think about that a moment. Every night I went to sleep wondering if tomorrow would see me killed for a crime that had not occurred — one that could not have occurred without the conniving of the local doctor. This should not have been possible. Habeas Corpus means produce the body. In my case that would have helped me. Justice itself had been defrauded shamefully.

I lost eighteen years to Death Row. My cousin, Fred, fared even worse. I beg you to remember him. Fred fell ill with malaria. We begged the guards to give him the medication that he needed. We were told that he was going to be executed, so why should they waste medication on him? Denied medication, he became weaker. On August 29th 1985 Fred died from complications arising out of the untreated illness. Fred Masembe was an undeniably innocent man, murdered through judicial neglect by a corrupt regime.

I later wrote a petition to the President asking him to exercise the prerogative of mercy. Bizarrely, the authorities accepted that 'the murder victim' Wandyaka was alive and well in 1989, but I remained on Death Row in the notorious Luzira Upper Prison until the turn of the new millennium. It was at this time that a committee investigating my innocence went to my home village. They asked about my general behaviour. The committee learnt that the man I was accused of killing was alive, but I did not receive any immediate response 'til July 29, 2000 when I was released. I had been on Death Row for eighteen years and Fred had been dead for almost fifteen of them—all this for a crime that never happened. It was a 'crime' that forensic pathology and even a modicum of an honest investigation could easily have resolved and prevented.

This book is welcome, and I recommend it. It is essential that forensic pathology, other forensic sciences, crime-scene investigations, and police investigations are integrated. If that had happened in my case, the terrible injustice that my late cousin and I suffered would never have happened. I hope that lessons are learned, not just in Britain—the main focus of this book—but internationally, especially in Uganda. My case should never have been allowed to happen, but my hopes are for the future. I want to see an end to the death penalty, but not just that. Preventable injustices, like the one that robbed me of almost two decades of my life, my wife, my innocent co-accused, Fred, and much more, should not be tolerated.

Impact of the Injustice on My Family

As you know my cousin Fred—my brother—with whom I was convicted and sentenced to death, died of malaria and complications in prison in 1985. His innocence has not been properly acknowledged, and nor has the consequences of his death. He was murdered by the neglect of a corrupt regime. My wife died after my conviction. My family paid a heavy price too. My children did not go to school because they lacked school fees—I had lost all my property and business, so I could not support them when they needed me most. It is not just the wrongly accused and/or convicted that suffer from these injustices. My children were innocent too, yet they lost the chance of an education because of this case. My health suffered too. I am now disabled and sick because of my living situation during imprisonment.

My Life Out of Prison

I have chosen to forgive everyone who falsely accused me. Wandyaka is now dead. He died fearing that I would come after him seeking revenge. I never wanted revenge, then or now. I wanted justice—still do. I want an end to the death penalty. I want a fair justice system. I want opportunities for my children, and those of Death Row inmates, and other prisoners too. I chose to do something about this.

I decided not to sue the government because it would affect forgiveness of other inmates, and because the original injustice was committed under another government. However, I remain dedicated to the causes I believe in. I participate in activities all over the world aimed at abolishing the death penalty and at preventing injustice. I visit my brothers and sisters on Death Row to encourage them, using my testimony to do so. I built a school to help the children of inmates, partly because my children missed school and that still hurts me a lot.

Books like this help to inform the public. I am happy to have been given the opportunity to tell my story. I hope that readers of this book will think about my case and my life and understand my struggle against the death penalty and injustice, and remember that forensic pathology could and should have prevented it. Imagine losing two decades of your life to Death Row, wondering if each day would be your last for murder when your 'victim' was alive and well. Can't happen? It happened to me and my cousin, the late Fred Masembe.

Foreword by Daryl Clemens[9]

At the start of the short story anthology ***'Unfettered'*** there is a foreword by Patrick Rothfuss, where he admits that he doesn't read forewords, isn't sure what they are for, and has no idea what to say. It's among the best things I've ever read. I'm definitely not him, but I too am not sure what to say. I'll give it my best shot, and you can decide if I hit the nail on the head or, if you'd rather, just skip ahead to the main body of this work and leave me to my personal musings.

I have been in the forensic science business for more than two decades. Things have changed a lot in that time. DNA was not really a thing when I started. Sure, it was out there, but it wasn't being done much yet. We made do with the old school serology of ABO types and blood markers. I can remember not collecting blood in some scenes, because we just weren't going to do anything with it. I can also remember the

9. Daryl Clemens is a Crime Scene Technician for the Forensic Services Unit of the Grand Rapids (MI) Police Department. He has been in law enforcement since 1993 and has been with Grand Rapids Police Department since 1994. Courses that he has attended include: Impression Evidence, Advanced Crime Scene Reconstruction, Bullet Trajectory Reconstruction, Police Cable Video Production, Bloodstain Pattern Analysis, Medicolegal Investigation of Death, Traffic Accident Investigation, Serology and Trace Evidence Collection, Forensic Light Sources, and Evidence Technician School. He has attended prestigious international events and courses too.

Clemens has been instructing courses on Crime Scene Investigation, Latent Print Processing, Photography and Shooting Scene Investigation for more than fifteen years. His publications include: *Bounce Lighting, Digital Photography as a Note Taking Tool, Pocket UV light, Technical Note: WetWop, Making 1:1 Images with Adobe Photoshop, An Unusual Accidental Death, A Bloodstain Pattern Calculator in C, Burglary Investigations*, and *An Introduction to Crime Scene Reconstruction for the Criminal Profiler*. He also created a video production, *Black Powder Processing* demonstrating the technique of processing with black fingerprint powder and the software, *MoreStains* which will calculate the angle and area of origin of a bloodstain. He has been interviewed by both Evidence Technology Magazine and Popular Photography Magazine.

He is on the board of **the International Crime Scene Investigators Association**, after spending more than 10 years as the editor of *The Examiner*, the association's newsletter. He is also the Editor of *Crime and Clues*, an on-line magazine devoted to Criminal Investigation and Forensic Science. Clemens is a member of the **International Association for Identification** (IAI) and a past member of both the **Midwestern Association of Forensic Scientists** (MAFS) and the **Association for Crime Scene Reconstruction** (ACSR).

early days of DNA when it was possible to not have enough sample in a visible blood stain. In fact, I show pictures in training of one scene from about 1998 where there is blood visible on a door frame, but the DNA tests came back negative — too degraded, not enough sample. We had to use blood from another source (location) in the crime-scene — carpet outside — to get a profile of our victim to place him back in the scene. I can remember not having swabs in the crime-scene kit, and using first aid gauze as a blood collection tool.

Forensic science used to be characterized by what my former partner sometimes called 'Cowboy Science'. This is similar to the 'Spilsburyism' you'll read about in later chapters. Back in the day, it was all about your status as an expert and how many trials you'd testified in and to an extent, once you were an expert, things were so — because you said they were. We've moved past that now, though more work remains to be done.

Forensic pathology is at the heart of every death investigation, and there can be no discounting the vital role the pathologist plays. TV shows focus on determining the 'time of death', which is generally never more than an estimate. Ask a pathologist for time of death, and they will ask — "when was the victim last seen alive?" and then, "when was the body discovered?" Time of death, they will tell you, is somewhere in between. Their real role is determining the cause and manner of death — ruling the death as to homicide, suicide, accidental or natural. This is sometimes complicated in the United States, as for years death investigation fell to the Coroner, who was elected and not required to be a doctor of any kind, let alone a pathologist. There are still Coroners in many places, though often they send questioned cases to be examined by a pathologist. Elsewhere, you will find a Medical Examiner system, where, generally speaking, the head is a forensic pathologist, though some of the scene investigators may not be doctors.

A death investigation is a machine with a lot of moving parts. It often includes emergency medical personnel, fire-fighters, police officers, detectives, supervisors, crime lab personnel and medical examiners. When everybody works together, things run smoothly. When some people start pursuing their own agenda, things can quickly run off the rails. It's easy to say that there should be no egos involved in an investigation, but everybody wants to feel like what they are doing matters. And, nobody likes to be wrong. Doctors, of course, are known for their egos. It's almost a med school graduation requirement.

I will note that there is clearly some cultural difference between the US and UK in that the author of this text suggests that the Pathologist should answer to the Police—specifically the chief investigator. This may be a consequence of Spilsburyism that occurred in the UK, and its effects there.[10] However, in the US, most people want exactly the opposite—the medical examiners and crime lab scientists removed from supervision by the police. There are pros and cons to doing things both ways.

The other question raised here is: 'What do we do when justice goes awry?' Like leaving egos at home, it's also easy to say that we should 'do everything that we can' in these cases, implying that we can, or should, actually attempt to do *everything*. There isn't enough time or money to ever do everything, and determining how much is enough is something every investigation struggles with. *Everything possible and everything reasonable are two very different things.*

---

10. To clarify, it was essential to confront the effects of Spilsburyism in Britain. It had set back investigations decades. That required investigations to come under the control of the SIO. However, the interests of police, criminal justice system, victims and defendants will inevitably diverge. All are important and need to be protected. The investigation should have a point of control, and that person would be held accountable for the course of the inquiry, usually through a court.

Under Spilsburyism, he took the laurels when it went right, but seldom the criticism if and when he got it wrong, and that system was passed down to his successors. On rare occasions where he was questioned, it was through opposing lawyers and experts—both of which are important counterbalances. They should not be bound by decisions taken by the SIO or Spilsburyesque forensic pathologist, and should question it. Between the two competing interests, the truth will usually lie: The author.

Dr Manock — the Australian Spilsbury

By Dr Bob Moles[11]

After completing his training as a medical doctor at Leeds University, Dr Colin Manock was appointed to the position of Chief Forensic Pathologist in South Australia in 1968. He remained in that position until he retired in 1995, having completed some 10,000 autopsies. He said he helped to secure over 400 criminal convictions.

During that time, he gave evidence in many cases which made no sense at all. In the case of Gerald Warren, he told the court in a murder trial that having the fabric of corduroy pressed against the skin would cause injuries indistinguishable from those inflicted by a blow from the threaded end of a metal pipe. He also said that falling out of a moving vehicle would cause similar injuries to those inflicted if a vehicle was driven over a person.

In the case of Terry Akritidis, he gave a time of death which was two hours after the boy's dead body had been found by the police. He said that the boy had no serious external injuries after falling from a considerable height onto a concrete roof because 'his clothing was interposed between his body and the surface that it struck'.

In Peter Marshall's case, he said that a man had struck his head after falling from his bed which explained the blood pooling around his head. The following day he found that he had been shot in the head, with a bullet lodged in his brain.

In the case of three babies aged less than one year, he gave the cause of death of each of them as bronchopneumonia. It was later discovered that they had no trace of such a lung infection. They had each been

11. Dr Moles is a widely published academic — he retains the copyright on this preface. His work can be seen at **Networked Knowledge**. He is also involved with **the Flinders University Miscarriages of Justice Project**.

severely beaten — one of them had 15 broken ribs, with severe bruising and a spinal injury. The Coroner found that Dr Manock's autopsy reports had achieved the opposite of their intended purpose — they closed off inquiries instead of opening them up. The Coroner found that Manock had been fundamentally incompetent and had given spurious (dishonest) answers to the Coroner at the Inquest into the babies' deaths. Remarkably, the Coroner then 'withheld' his report whilst Dr Manock gave evidence at the trial of Henry Keogh.

Keogh had been charged with the murder of his fiancée by drowning her in the domestic bath at their home in 1994. The Coroner released his report on the baby deaths two days after Keogh was convicted. During Keogh's twenty years in prison, Manock had been questioned about his work in Keogh's case before the Medical Board. In that inquiry he retracted significant elements of his expert findings which he had confidently given at Keogh's trial. Remarkably, it still was not possible to get the case referred back to the Court of Appeal.

The Australian appeal provisions had been modelled on the Criminal Appeal Act 1907 (UK) — and unlike the UK had remained unamended since enacted. With no right to a further appeal and with no Criminal Review Commission, we persuaded the Australian Human Rights Commission that the Australian appeal rights were in breach of Australia's international human rights obligations. They issued a report to that effect to the South Australian parliament which then legislated to create a new statutory right of appeal with effect from May 2013 — a right which has since been taken up also in Tasmania.

When Keogh applied to the court for leave to appeal in 2013, he was then provided with a forensic report which had been obtained by the Solicitor-General in 2004 which had stated that the forensic evidence had been misinterpreted. It did not support a murder scenario, but only a faint and fall accident. No one has yet explained why the report was not disclosed earlier. On Keogh's appeal, the court found that Manock's evidence concerning the 'mechanism of murder' was 'false and misleading' and had no scientific basis to it at all — just as the Coroner had found all those years ago in the baby deaths cases.

Since then the 1973 case of Frits Van Beelen was heard by the appeal court. In that case, Manock had determined a precise time for the death of a young girl by a visual inspection of her stomach contents after they had been kept in frozen storage for three months. Again, the court found that there was no scientific basis to Manock's finding of time of death, but the judges disagreed about whether the conviction should be overturned.

Perhaps the most surprising finding of all was discovered when reviewing an early civil action which Dr Manock had with his employer about his conditions of employment. During that litigation (1972–1978) the head of the forensic science centre (and the State of South Australia) gave sworn evidence to say that Dr Manock was not properly qualified to conduct a forensic autopsy on his own. They said he had no proper training in histopathology which was said to be an essential component of a complete autopsy. They also added that although he was in an expert's position, he had no expert qualifications. That would mean that he would not then have been qualified to give evidence as an expert witness in criminal proceedings. That would mean that on each occasion when he subsequently appeared in criminal proceedings and stated that he was qualified as an expert witness, that too was false and misleading—which means that all of those convictions should be overturned.

South Australia is now faced with the unenviable task of reviewing more than 400 criminal convictions and 10,000 autopsies. Whilst prosecutors appear unwilling to acknowledge the scale of the disaster, the appeal of Derek Bromley, an aboriginal man who is still in prison after 35 years could and should have been a game-changer. His appeal was heard in 2018. Despite accepting that Manock was once again wrong in attributing drowning as the cause of death—it is now listed as undetermined—the appeal court refused to overturn Bromley's conviction. He has passed his non-parole period and remains in prison because he will not admit guilt.[12]

12. For further details of these cases see the article on **Institutional Reform in South Australia** available at http://netk.net.au/SA/SA15.pdf and also see **Networked Knowledge** at http://netk.net.au or contact Dr Bob Moles at bobmoles@iprimus.com.au

PART ONE

SPILSBURYISM

"Spilsbury's statements in the witness box were often based on insufficient material, and a lack of clinical experience".

Professor Michael Green

CHAPTER 1

Limitations

Importance

Forensic pathology is undoubtedly a very important science, but one that is surrounded by misunderstanding of both its significance and limitations. It has always been this way. It cannot, for example, tell you precisely when a murder took place. There are far too many variables to enable anything more than a range of times that death occurred within. There are however, several indicators that should be established and not just the obvious ones such as body weight, body temperature, ambient temperature and the progress of rigor mortis. Analysis of stomach contents and of the rate of dissipation of alcohol content in the body can assist in establishing a likely range for when death occurred too.

However, despite ongoing research, no science can give a precise time of death — yet. Previously, forensic pathology's function was thought to be determining the cause of death, but this was a very narrow interpretation and not what SIOs required. They needed to piece together the events that led to the death in question. Forensic pathology certainly had a part to play in that, but that would require reorganisation of the role of forensic pathologists and the system that they worked under.

The Real Question

Important as it undoubtedly is, forensic pathology has been a controversial science for several decades. At least some of the problems that have blighted modern forensic pathology — and still do — were also issues a century ago when Sir William Wilcox was at the height of his power and his protégé Sir Bernard Spilsbury, the first forensic pathologist to become famous, was making his name. Their style of giving evidence was similar. Neither could brook opposition and neither could bring themselves to admit error. Any concession was couched in the virtually meaningless expression: "It is possible". That hardly assisted the jury.

The real question was 'Is it likely?' rather than 'Is it possible?' So in reality the 'concession' offered in evidence by Wilcox and later Spilsbury was little more than a grudging means of countering any potential or actual damage done to their opinion by giving the implied suggestion that while it was possible, it was not likely and could therefore be discounted by the jury. That suited the prosecution, whose job it was to secure convictions and both Wilcox and Spilsbury knew why the prosecution wanted them rather than other experts—they were hugely effective witnesses who juries trusted. More often than not they delivered the opinion, and later, evidence that those hiring them wanted, but there was a price to pay—an enormous one.

CHAPTER 2

Bridging the Gap

Crippen

Wilcox and, even more so, Spilsbury were able to bridge the gap between experts and ordinary people by making their evidence easy for juries to understand. This was a crucial skill as they won their trust, sometimes against the weight of evidence. The young Spilsbury made his name by taking microscopic slides in the notorious case of Hawley Harvey Crippen. Spilsbury provided the proof that the remains, said to be those of Cora Crippen, were those of Crippen's missing wife by showing that there was an abdominal scar on the body.

The defence witnesses stuck to their opinions, but Spilsbury's testimony had severely damaged their credibility. Crippen was convicted and hanged in 1911. Recent DNA tests suggested that Spilsbury's slides contained male DNA. Obviously, that would have destroyed the case against Crippen and with it Spilsbury's reputation before he had made his name.

Star Status

Post Crippen, Spilsbury went from strength to strength. His star status made it nigh on impossible to challenge him. His opinion, once given, had been set in stone. Nothing could change it — not even facts. It is clear from analysis of his work conducted by others that he was prone to allowing his testimony to go beyond the limits of his science and for his personal prejudices to trump the interests of justice.[1] That should never be tolerated from any expert, no matter her or his standing.

However, Spilsbury's hubris cut both ways. It could send possibly innocent people to the gallows or it could save the likely guilty from that fate

1. This review of Andrew Rose's book **Lethal Witness: Sir Bernard Spilsbury, Honorary Pathologist** at http://www.telegraph.co.uk/culture/books/non_fictionreviews/3667415/An-over-celebrated-pathologist.html gives a flavour of the controversial pathologist's methods.

and it could achieve either without necessarily having the evidence to support his conclusions. Such reliance on expert testimony is dangerous, especially as there was no need for it. Spilsbury was an impressive witness, but he was not infallible and his inability to contemplate the possibility that he could be wrong, resulted in him rigidly sticking to an opinion no matter what. He was far from alone in this failing—one that sadly finds an echo in expert witnesses decades later, such as Michael Heath. Dr Heath was forced to confront his hubris and eventually discovered humility, as he avoided a bid at the General Medical Council to strike him off (remove him from the profession).

CHAPTER 3

Second to None?

Worthy Opponents

In his day, Professor Spilsbury's reputation was second to none, sending many to the gallows. Some of Spilsbury's cases were the most famous of his time, but controversy lurked not far from the surface.[1] Crippen, Frederick Seddon, George Joseph Smith, Major Herbert Rowse Armstrong and Alfred Arthur Rouse all went to the gallows on Spilsbury's say so, but perhaps the most important of Spilsbury's victims was a far less well known one — Norman Thorne — executed for a crime he may well have been innocent of (see **Chapter 3: The Martyr to Spilsburyism** in our forthcoming publication **Forensic Pathology — Righting Wrongs**). That may have applied to Sidney Fox as well — Professor Sydney Smith certainly thought so. While the Thorne case damaged Spilsbury's reputation — it deserved to — Spilsbury survived the furore, but perceptions changed and had begun to do so even in his lifetime among his peers at least.

Professors Robert Brontë and Smith proved worthy opponents, but Spilsbury's reputation tended to carry greater weight with judges and juries. Spilsbury was disparaging towards Brontë, referring to him as 'that man'. Brontë disputed Spilsbury's findings, but never his standing within the science. Spilsbury was a larger than life figure in forensic pathology during his lifetime. He helped to make forensic pathology respectable — previously it was known as 'the Beastly Profession' — and solved many mysteries, combining an ability to simplify the science for juries and court publicity while seeming to avoid it and also develop investigative techniques. His mentor Wilcox had done the same, but so had Smith and arguably Smith's mentor too, Professor Harvey Littlejohn. Smith and Littlejohn adopted different methods to investigation and in

1. For further information on Spilsbury see http://www.ncbi.nlm.nih.gov/pmc/articles/PMC3037214/

giving evidence, but where they clashed, Spilsbury tended to come out on top, even though Smith had the cold comfort of probably being right.

Spilsbury for the Defence

In one case Spilsbury made a rare appearance for the defence—it resulted in a not proven verdict. Smith ruefully predicted that it would not be the last that was heard of 'young Merrett'. Sadly, Smith was right. John Donald Merrett got away with probably murdering his mother—the evidence suggests that he did—and forged an extensive career in crime, culminating in a double murder of his estranged wife and her mother, before committing suicide (see **Chapter 6: Freed to Kill** in our forthcoming publication **Forensic Pathology—Righting Wrongs**). Merrett wasn't the only killer that Spilsbury's evidence had helped to avoid the gallows.

Harold Loughan was a villain—no doubt about it—but was he a murderer? Spilsbury concluded that he was not physically capable of strangling Rose Robinson, the landlady of the John Barleycorn pub in Portsmouth on November 28th 1943. Loughan had a deformed right hand, which consisted of three stubs and two complete fingers. The Crown's pathologist, a young Keith Simpson, was convinced that the marks were consistent with such a deformed hand. Spilsbury's opinion that Loughan could not have strangled Robinson using that hand as it was not strong enough and could not get sufficient grip to strangle Robinson was formed partly on the basis of Loughan's weak hand-shake. However, Loughan had a very powerful incentive to deceive Spilsbury into thinking his grip was weaker than it actually was. His very life was at stake.

Loughan had been arrested for robberies. He confessed to those and also to Robinson's murder. He retracted his confession, claiming that the police had put words into his mouth. Loughan seemed to have an intention to mess the police around, especially as he knew that he had a powerful alibi. Five people said he had been in an air raid shelter in London at the time of the murder, which had occurred miles away in Portsmouth. Nevertheless, the prosecutor Joshua Casswell KC was convinced that Loughan's confession was true. Casswell had made his name as a defence attorney—he knew the ropes. Just two years before the murder of Rose Robinson, Casswell secured the acquittal of Mabel Attrill for the murder of Frank Cave in Gosport on the Isle of Wight. There was no question that Attrill had shot Cave. The issue was whether the gun had gone off accidentally. Casswell argued that the prosecution had failed to meet its burden, as the House of Lords — then the highest court in the land — had decided a very similar case six years previously by requiring the prosecution to disprove that it was an accident. Casswell showed that the prosecution had not done so. It took the jury ten minutes to acquit Attrill. Casswell was an able and experienced silk.

An Enigmatic Case

But Loughan's was an enigmatic case — alibi versus confession — that remains controversial even now. He got lucky at his trials. The jury could not agree a verdict at the first trial in Winchester and the second at the Old Bailey resulted in an acquittal. Spilsbury was an important part of the jigsaw. He rarely appeared for the defence and despite his clearly waning powers he was still the great Sir Bernard. Loughan was quickly arrested and convicted of another attempted murder. Several crimes, convictions and sentences later Casswell had his say about the prolific criminal Loughan, in memoirs that *The People* serialised. Casswell was clearly no fool — his superb defence of Attrill proved that.

He had had a distinguished career at the Bar, and Loughan's case still grated with him years later. In Casswell's opinion, Loughan had got away with murder. Loughan sued *The People* for defamation, claiming that he was being called a murderer, even though he had been acquitted and was therefore entitled to be presumed innocent. He was entitled to that presumption of innocence, but both Casswell and *The People* were entitled to free speech and they had exercised it under the shield of justification — the truth is a complete defence to defamation actions. *The People* and Casswell had the evidence and Loughan's star witness, Spilsbury had been dead for over fifteen years. Loughan's action was gleefully opposed. Loughan had foolishly opened the door to being tried again, but on a lower standard of proof — the balance of probabilities. All that had to be proved was that it was more likely than not that Loughan had indeed murdered Rose Robinson. The libel jury found that it was not libellous to say that. He subsequently confessed to *The People*, saying that he was dying. Less than two years later Loughan died of cancer. Sir Bernard had been wrong about Loughan.

CHAPTER 4

The Other Side

Friends in High Places

Less than a decade before Rose Robinson was murdered by Loughan, Spilsbury experienced the other side — helplessness in the face of a suspect who seemed to have a charmed life. This suspect was protected by friends in high places, or so it seemed. On June 17th 1934, parts of the dismembered body of a young woman, who was five months pregnant, had been discovered in Brighton train station. She was dubbed 'Pretty Feet' as they were deemed to be those of a dancer when her lower limbs were discovered in a trunk at King's Cross Station in London. Her head and arms were never recovered. This made identification of the victim impossible — at least then. Nevertheless, some clues caused police, led by Chief Inspector Ronald Donaldson to identify a prime suspect, aided by Spilsbury.

Abortions were illegal at that time, but there were more than just the dangerous back-street abortionists on offer. It was an open secret that Dr Edward Massiah performed abortions, but he had influential friends, or so it was believed. He was the prime suspect in the murder of 'Pretty Feet', but despite both police and Spilsbury believing that she was murdered by an abortion practitioner — Donaldson was convinced that Massiah was responsible and put him under covert surveillance — the doctor never stood trial. Spilsbury was known for his strong anti-abortion views — his notes confirmed Donaldson's suspicions — but Massiah had influential connections. Even when a woman died in London as a result of an abortion Massiah carried out there, he was not prosecuted. This murder — 'Pretty Feet' — was never solved, but it led to the discovery of another trunk murder and once again Spilsbury was instructed.

Fortunate

Violette Kaye had been missing since an argument with her boyfriend Cecil England (better known as Toni Mancini) on May 10th 1934. The stench coming from an abode that Mancini had taken near Brighton Train Station was unpleasant and overpowering. The inquiry into the other Trunk Murder led to the discovery of Kaye's remains. Mancini had obviously sent a telegram to Kaye's sister from Brighton, saying that she had taken a job in Paris and would write soon. She was already dead. After being questioned by police over Kaye's disappearance Mancini fled Brighton, leaving the trunk containing the decomposing remains of Kaye behind. He was later arrested in London and stood trial for Kaye's murder in December 1934 at Lewes Assizes. James Cassells KC prosecuted. Armed with proof that Mancini had sent the false telegram and the formidable Spilsbury, Cassells was confident of securing a conviction. Mancini was defended by Norman Birkett KC, who argued that one of Kaye's clients—she was a prostitute—was the real killer and that Mancini, believing that his criminal record would count against him, panicked.

Spilsbury had no doubt that Mancini was the murderer, but for once Spilsbury's reputation was not enough for the jury. Birkett managed to create a doubt in the jury's mind by focusing on Kaye's profession and undermining the forensic science. It worked. Mancini was acquitted after just over two hours. In 1976, down on his luck, Mancini followed Loughan's example by confessing to a newspaper, *The News of the World*. A prosecution for perjury was considered—it was all that could have been done at the time, but Mancini died soon afterwards anyway. Both Loughan and Mancini knew that their confessions could not be used against them as double jeopardy[1] applied. Those confessions were made before it became illegal to profit from crimes. It is still unclear if either Loughan or Mancini profited from their admissions to the media, but Loughan lost his libel action and was therefore labelled a murderer.

Usually, Spilsbury was on the other side. Norman Thorne was far from the only person who had been Splisburyed.[2]

---

1. In certain circumstances prosecutors can now have a second bite of the cherry if new evidence, such as DNA, emerges.
2. For further information on Thorne's case and its implications see the following chapter and **Chapter 3: The Martyr to Spilsburyism** in **Forensic Pathology—Righting Wrongs** (forthcoming).

CHAPTER 5

The Price of Spilsburyism

Expertise

Norman Thorne coined a phrase that offers a stark warning of the risks of poor science and over-reliance on reputations, built on false foundations. "I am a martyr to Spilsburyism", Thorne wrote to his father days before he was hanged for a crime that probably never occurred. Suicide was at least a possibility even if it suited Thorne's convenience that his erstwhile fiancé Elsie Cameron was dead. Thorne was alleged to have strangled her. Nevertheless, Thorne had been forced to counter Spilsburyism with both arms tied behind his back and it cost him his life. It provided cold comfort that this was the turning point against Spilsburyism, if not with juries, then among some distinguished peers of his profession. Many believed then as now that the case against Thorne had not been proved beyond all reasonable doubt. Spilsbury deserved strong criticism over Thorne's case and he got it, but there was plenty of blame to go round.

The defence experts had to cope with a situation that was hardly their fault, but it had the effect of making it impossible to challenge Spilsbury's conclusions as comprehensively as they deserved to be. If the coffin had been closed efficiently, as it should have been, decomposition would have been considerably slower. If Britain had stored bodies as efficiently as other European jurisdictions had since the 1890s, the level of decomposition would have been nowhere near as advanced as it was in this case. If that had happened, Spilsbury's unsupported opinions would have been capable of resolution, as decomposition would not have been an issue. Foul play or not, Thorne was not responsible for that, but with his life at stake, there was no redress beyond scoring points on the shoddy procedure — hardly an adequate alternative under the circumstances. The Court of Appeal refused an expert panel to resolve the medical issues. Shamefully, evidence that may have helped to prove innocence was allowed to rot — literally.

Spilsburyism

There were ample grounds to doubt Spilsbury's conclusions. Eminent experts disagreed with him. Against them was the man the judge frequently referred to as 'the greatest living pathologist'. Mr Justice (Sir William) Finlay was a comparatively new judge. Appointed in 1924, he presided over Thorne's trial in March 1925—but such a glowing recommendation must have had an inappropriate effect upon the jury. The judge's view that Spilsbury was right and the defence experts were wrong must have come over loud and clear. Nevertheless, the Court of Appeal, headed by the then Lord Chief Justice, Baron (Gordon) Hewitt, dismissed the pleas of defence KC James Cassells that the dispute over the medical evidence should be considered by an independent panel of experts. Thorne was hanged on April 22nd 1925, just a few weeks after his trial.

Over twenty years later, Thorne's nemesis was dead, but while Thorne paid the highest price, a year after Thorne's martyrdom to Spilsburyism, the eminent pathologist appears to have been involved in another miscarriage of justice. This time Spilsbury appeared for the defence. His evidence helped the despicable John Donald Merrett to probably get away with the murder of his mother for financial gain. Merrett took advantage of his good fortune by going on to commit numerous crimes, which culminated in the double murder of his wife and mother-in-law. A few days later, while wanted on suspicion of their murder, Merrett committed suicide.

Forensic science, which obviously includes forensic pathology, should have no side. While Spilsbury occasionally appeared for defendants—his status as a Home Office pathologist restricted his room for manoeuvre, although that did not apply in Scotland due to its separate criminal justice system—he famously seems to have got Merrett's case spectacularly wrong there. At the very least, the fortunate defendant went on to use his good luck to carve himself a niche in the annals of crime, with offences ranging from smuggling to fraud and many more, liberally interspersed with imprisonment before avoiding a likely appointment with the hangman by committing suicide. In fact, Spilsbury appeared for the defence at least once more in Harold Loughan's case and he got that wrong too. These forays into defence work were far from Spilsbury's finest hours.[1]

Spilsbury avoided awkward questions over Loughan in his lifetime as the eminent pathologist was long dead by the time the career criminal confessed that Casswell, and not Spilsbury, had been right about the murder of Rose Robinson. The same applied over Donald Merrett, aka Ronald Chesney, as Merrett's long criminal career came to an abrupt end almost seven years after Spilsbury took his own life.

1. See the previous chapter and also **Chapter 6: Freed to Kill?** in **Forensic Pathology—Righting Wrongs (Fitted-In Project**, forthcoming).

CHAPTER 6

Spilsburyed

The Dangers of Spilsburyism

His fame had made him all but untouchable during his life-time—even opponents as eminent as Professor Smith found juries and even judges tended to prefer Spilsburyism. He helped to make forensic pathology a respectable profession. He is even seen as using crime-scene investigation techniques before the term CSI was coined, but it came at too high a price. Spilsbury was inflexible and arrogant. Norman Thorne may not have been the only defendant to go to the gallows a 'Martyr to Spilsburyism'. Even now almost a century after he made his name, Spilsbury polarises opinion. Opposing experts seemed to be on a hiding to nothing even if the science was actually on their side. Smith was one of the experts hired by Sidney Fox's defence. Spilsbury was adamant that the deceased—Fox's mother Rosaline—had been strangled. Spilsbury accepted that the hyoid bone had not been broken but insisted that he had detected a bruise at the back of the larynx. Spilsbury even accepted that when Smith and another expert examined it the bruise was no longer there. The only evidence that it had ever been there was Spilsbury's word. It was enough for the jury. Fox was hanged in April 1930. Smith was convinced that Fox, who had numerous faults, was innocent of the murder of his mother despite strong circumstantial evidence.[1] But the dangers of Spilsburyism were even more pervasive.

1. There is no question that there was a strong circumstantial case against Fox. He was a swindler. Both he and his mother were involved in those crimes. The fire-related evidence showed that there were no traces of soot in her, indicating that she was not breathing when the fire was raging, but that also meant that the fire had not killed her. The timing of her death was incredibly convenient for Fox—just before a life insurance policy on her was due to lapse.

   That Fox was a rogue was not in doubt, but was he a murderer? The only evidence capable of amounting to proof was the bruise on the larynx and even Spilsbury accepted that it was not there when Smith and his fellow forensic pathologist, Robert Brontë, examined it. The only evidence that it had ever been there was Spilsbury's insistence. That should never have been accepted as evidence, let alone secured a conviction, which cost a man—rogue or not—his life.

Unscientific Spilsburyism

Spilsbury was strong in his opinions, but on at least two occasions he appears to have allowed his political prejudice to trump actual evidence. In 1923 he was even prepared to allow a gay soldier, Albert Dearnley, to go to the gallows for the murder of another soldier, James Ellis, against the evidence because he disapproved of homosexuality. Ellis had masochistic tendencies. Although Dearnley had told inconsistent accounts — homosexuality was illegal at the time — the accused may have been convinced that the truth would get him hanged, so he lied and lied. Ellis was found dead with his hands tied behind his back and his feet behind his knees and he was gagged. Ellis suffocated, but was it deliberate? It was obvious that someone else was involved and that person was Dearnley. The evidence suggested that it was a bondage game that had gone wrong — what would now be termed auto-erotic asphyxiation. However, over 90 years ago Dearnley's lies had done him no favours, but the forensic pathology had a story to tell — one that Spilsbury chose not to. Dearnley was convicted of murder in Winchester on November 23rd 1923 and sentenced to death. It would soon become clear that he didn't deserve it, even in terms of the times.

Spilsbury suspected that Ellis' death was an accident — he was far too gifted a pathologist not to have at least suspected the truth, but he allowed his prejudice against homosexuality to secure his silence, knowing that it could cost Dearnley his life over an accident. The truth came out accidentally due to a letter Dearnley had written to a girlfriend — he was perhaps bisexual or concealing his homosexuality. That letter caused the prison Governor to suspect that something was wrong. The Governor obtained a stay of execution and the truth came out that Ellis' death was a bondage session gone wrong, rather than murder. Dearnley's application for leave to appeal had been dismissed in December 1923, but the Home Secretary, Viscount William Bridgeman, commuted the death sentence in January 1924 after the Governor's intervention.

Dave Barclay was not impressed with Spilsbury's conduct in Dearnley's case. "Well if that's the case, that's obviously wrong, so he shouldn't have done that", Barclay said. "In fact, nowadays, I would expect all the pathologists to be actively seeking for things like that, because that's one of the traditional things. Auto-erotic asphyxiation is very well recognised now. It probably wasn't quite so well recognised in those days".

However, that wasn't the only time that Spilsbury's views—prejudices—trumped evidence. A 14 year-old had been raped by soldiers, causing three doctors to recommend an abortion for the victim's safety. Spilsbury's virulently anti-abortion views resulted in him giving evidence that was, at best, ludicrous in an infamous case in 1938. Dr Alec Bourne, who conducted the abortion, which was illegal at the time, was the high-profile defendant. Scandalously, Spilsbury claimed there was no risk to the rape victim by forcing her to carry the foetus to term and that he knew of a child as young as nine who had given birth without danger. This time Spilsbury's aura had slipped. The jury quickly acquitted Bourne and Spilsbury's reputation took a fully deserved hit. Five years later he got the murder of Rose Robinson spectacularly wrong.

Perhaps fearing exposure and disgrace as his powers waned, Spilsbury took his own life in 1947. He is now seen by the retired forensic pathologist, Professor Bernard Knight, as 'a very dangerous man'. Thorne's denunciation of Spilsburyism was years ahead of his time, but today's expert witnesses must also be aware of the consequences of one of the legacies of Spilsburyism—inflexibility in their evidence and an aura of expert witnesses that allows their status to trump actual evidence.

CHAPTER 7

Passing the Baton

Pre-eminence

Sir Bernard Spilsbury was the pre-eminent expert of his era. He towered over his profession. Due to this, the dangers were immense. Spilsbury was near impossible to challenge and those that dared to almost always came off second best. Being right was cold comfort. Spilsbury had an aura that trumped evidence and even his science. Juries were often under his sway, which could and did lead to preventable errors often with the direst of consequences.

"So that's one danger and secondly, it's inevitable if everybody says you're terrific all the time, you begin to think you *are* terrific and you take short cuts and so on and that's what happened to Spilsbury and also he began to get old too", Professor Dave Barclays says.[1] "He wasn't totally au fait with all the latest scientific techniques and so on. I don't think Spilsbury would have happened now".

However, the problems remained and even posed other questions. Professor Sir William Wilcox had enjoyed pre-eminence too and saw challenge of his opinions as tantamount to an attack on his reputation. Spilsbury was certainly of that ilk too. Professor Sir Sydney Smith and his own mentor Professor Harvey Littlejohn challenged the pair, providing much needed opposition at trials — in practice the only form of peer-review Spilsbury was subjected to. Spilsbury's lack of respect for colleagues who opposed him, and pre-eminent status contributed to the problems faced by the next generation too, but that is only part of the story.

1. Barclay was the former Head of Physical Evidence at the National Crime Faculty. (NCF) He helped to develop the current procedures that integrated forensic pathology into the requirements of modern investigative practices, under the auspices of the Senior Investigating Officer (SIO).

Accountability

The methods of holding pathologists responsible were few and far between at that time. In practice it was limited to court proceedings, meaning that the opinions of judges and juries were decisive. Back then it could mean the difference between life and death. This was far from the best means of evaluating forensic pathologists and the effectiveness of their work, but in Spilsbury's day it was this or nothing. And Spilsbury had mastered the art of giving evidence. Juries liked and trusted him, as did judges. Why would he change the habits of a lifetime when they were so effective? Wilcox hadn't either and they had proved very effective too. As Professor Barclay says, "Because they were the pre-eminent experts, they weren't challenged. Other experts, even when they did challenge them, the jury could say, 'Well it's Spilsbury; he must be right', and that wasn't always the case, so that's one danger".

But it was a major danger and not just with Spilsbury. The system of holding forensic pathologists accountable was fundamentally flawed especially in Spilsbury's day, but it was bequeathed to his successors and their's too. Another was the individualistic view of forensic pathologists. With or without pre-eminence in their profession, they tended to be lone wolves. They did not see themselves as part of a team with police, scene of crime officers (SOCOs) and other forensic scientists. They also failed to appreciate the need for an integrated approach to investigations and casework.

"One of the problems with pathology was that not only didn't they see themselves as part of a team, but many of them saw themselves as a sole practitioner", Barclay says. "They were the only person that was doing it and they sometimes got defensive if somebody criticised them, because most of the time the only time they were criticised was in court by a pathologist working for the defence.

What should have happened is that somebody should have raised those issues with them before the report was actually finalised. They could have come together and actually agreed, 'Oh well actually, another explanation for it might be this, whatever', so if they hadn't thought of it, they got defensive when they went to court".

Barclay's approach was not considered in Spilsbury's day and when the baton was passed from Spilsbury and to a lesser extent Smith to Francis Camps, Keith Simpson and Donald Teare, the problems remained. Peer-review was unheard of. As the Three Musketeers inherited the baton, they kept each other in check to some extent as none of them achieved undisputed pre-eminence over their colleagues. They were, however, the only experts of sufficient standing to oppose each other, but Simpson achieved a degree of eminence, perhaps by virtue of his longevity — Camps died in 1972. Their competition avoided the pre-eminence issue that Wilcox and Spilsbury had enjoyed, but adversarial trials remained the only means of holding forensic pathology accountable. The obvious flaw in this remained — it could only correct mistakes after some damage had been done. Adversarial trials and inquests did not deliver accountability, nor were those processes designed to, as errors continued to occur and sometimes they had dire consequences. Spilsbury's successors proved far from immune to these dangers.

PART TWO

SECOND GENERATION

"If you can't prove it, don't claim it".

Professor Bernard Knight

CHAPTER 8

All for One and None for All

Reputations

With Spilsbury gone and Professor Smith approaching the end of his illustrious career, the next generation received the baton. Francis Camps, Keith Simpson and Donald Teare — the Three Musketeers — were the new leading lights of the profession. Nobody else had the authority to challenge them. Simpson was a protégé of Professor Smith. At first Camps, Simpson and Teare seemed friendly — even working together — but as their careers progressed they drifted apart, especially Camps. It was to some extent inevitable as the nature of the adversarial system meant that they were bound to oppose each other in court, just as Spilsbury and Brontë had done. When that crossed over into taking personal offence if an expert had the temerity to dare to oppose him, even when he was wrong, as Spilsbury did, professional courtesy was one of many casualties, but far from the most important.

The 1950s were to be the start of their era of pre-eminence and that led to their rivalry heating up. By the end of their careers all three were recognised for their achievements and rightly so. Camps had been given a head start in 1945 as he was recruited to run London Hospital Medical College's Department of Forensic Medicine, which Camps used to modernise forensic pathology. Camps recognised that other disciplines were important too. He was a forerunner of an integrated approach, having brought experts of other specialisms together in his department. Camps was a workaholic, but had a tendency to rub people up the wrong way. Some believed he courted publicity, but nobody could dispute his abilities.

Profile

Camps played a major part in bringing a suspected serial killer to trial. Long before the awful Dr Harold Shipman had qualified, another doctor, John Bodkin Adams, was suspected of being a prolific serial killer rather than an upholder of the Hippocratic Oath. There were over 160 suspicious deaths of his patients and 132 of them had made Adams a beneficiary. The expert evidence was the only way to prove murder, but Adams was acquitted at his first trial and the judge halted another due to an abuse of process. Adams was subsequently convicted of prescription fraud and other offences and removed from the Medical Register in 1957—the same year as his trials. He was reinstated in 1961.

Adams died in 1983 and is widely believed to have been one of the most prolific serial killers in British history. He was litigious too, winning libel actions against various media. In the 1950s the psychological motivation of serial killers was not understood as it is today. This was certainly a case that could have benefited from an integrated approach. Adams was an avaricious man, but there was more to his actions than just greed. Certainly, judge and jury were not satisfied with the financial motive, but if they had known the extent of him becoming a beneficiary of the deaths of his patients, they may have reached different conclusions. But Adams wasn't the only killer Camps testified against who cheated justice.

Camps had no shortage of high profile cases, such as the murder of Stanley Setty. The flamboyant Setty was killed by a business associate, Brian Donald Hume, in 1949—the business was 'shady' as both Setty and Hume knew. Despite seemingly compelling evidence, Hume was acquitted of murder the following year, but convicted of lesser offences—he had mutilated the body and dumped portions from an aircraft. Camps was certainly one of the leading authorities in his profession and appeared for the prosecution in Hume's case. Teare appeared for Hume's defence. Camps showed that Setty had lost a large amount of blood at Hume's place. After his acquittal of murder, the prosecution declined to try him a second time, so Hume pleaded guilty to lesser offences. He got away with murder. Being right was little consolation for Camps. Hume was released in 1958 for good behaviour, and then sold his confession to a newspaper. He had been fortunate to escape conviction for murder in Britain. He would not be so lucky in Switzerland.[1]

1. Quickly in need of more money Hume robbed a bank in London, but the money didn't go far, so he decided to rob a bank in Zurich. It did not go according to plan. The alarm was raised and he was chased out of the bank after shooting a teller. The teller survived. Bystanders chased him and a taxi-driver, Arthur Maag, tried to apprehend him. Hume shot him. Maag subsequently died. Hume was convicted and sentenced to life with hard labour. He was deported back to Britain in 1976 and was sent to Broadmoor Psychiatric Hospital for fifteen years.

CHAPTER 9

Cause Célèbre

The Wigwam Murder

Both Simpson and Teare felt that Camps was the instigator of tensions between them, but Simpson had at least one early skeleton in his closet. It was when he was a young man and probably did not affect guilt or innocence. It was however a cause célèbre — the Wigwam Murder of Joan Wolfe in September 1942.[1] Wolfe was last seen alive on September 14th 1942. Her relationship with August Sangret, a First Inhabitant Canadian soldier, lasted 81 days before ending tragically. Wolfe was murdered and Sangret paid for the crime with his life. Wolfe's remains were discovered on October 7th — rats had fed on her remains. Dr Eric Gardner, pathologist to the Coroner of Surrey, attended the scene with Scotland Yard's Detective Inspector Edward Greeno and Simpson. The remains were heavily decomposed and maggot-infested.

Simpson's examination revealed that death was likely to have occurred in mid-September which coincided with the date Wolfe was last seen alive. He also reconstructed her skull from the fragments, establishing the impact site where Wolfe had been struck probably with a bar or bough. Stab wounds were detected, including defensive injuries and at least one to the head had been caused by a distinctive weapon. A search of the area revealed important evidence against Sangret, including a blood stained bough and a distinctive knife, which was consistent with causing a parrot-beak shaped wound to Wolfe's skull.

Discrepancies?

Professor Dave Barclay is concerned with prevention. The system that he helped to introduce achieves that, but what about the past — cases like

1. Wolfe was a teenager when she first left home. Her mother was unable to cater for her. She naïvely drifted into relationships. Her's was a story that was unlikely to end well and it did not. She had been abandoned by one Canadian soldier before meeting August Sangret. Their relationship off and on lasted less than three months. Sangret built a wigwam for her so they would have somewhere to meet.

Sangret? "Well it can't redress problems in the past, because you'd have to do a retrospective review", he says. "I think there's absolutely no chance of people doing that because it would be so expensive for the reward. When do you stop either? Do you stop with the Wigwam murder from 1942[2]—nowadays you'd say, 'Whoa'! Where do you stop?"

But what if there are lessons to be learned even from cases that far back? Sangret was interviewed at length—it took days to write out, but while Sangret did not incriminate himself and he was released, the discovery of the knife was enough to charge him. Sangret stood trial. It took the jury just two hours to convict him. Sangret insisted that he was innocent. A strong recommendation for mercy from the jury failed to impress Home Secretary Herbert Morrison, who found the recommendation incomprehensible. Sangret was hanged on April 29th 1943. Circumstantial case or not, Greeno later wanted it acknowledged that Sangret had admitted his guilt just before he died.

The case remains controversial due to the methods used and the conclusions drawn by Simpson. "From what I've read, I'm absolutely certain that he was probably guilty, but the things that were said in evidence look almost completely unjustified", said Barclay, "and the blood grouping was 1:20 or less, or something like that was regarded as being conclusive, like Lynette White where 1 in 3800 was regarded as being conclusive and that was equally wrong, or more wrong".

Meanwhile, Camps made sure that both Simpson and Teare knew that he was in charge on the one that really mattered—10 Rillington Place—the case of the supposedly respectable John Christie, who had been exposed as a depraved serial killer. Christie was clearly a viable suspect just as Timothy Evans had claimed three years earlier. While Teare had been the pathologist on the Evans case, Camps had been called when Christie's crimes emerged in 1953.

2. August Sangret was a Canadian soldier of First Inhabitant birth. He was executed for the September 1942 murder of Joan Wolfe in Surrey. Professor Keith Simpson—one of the Three Musketeers—was the pathologist. Wolfe's body was badly decomposed at the time of discovery. Maggots had colonised her remains and flies were everywhere. Simpson revised his initial range for the time of death, which coincided with the time of her disappearance. Although forensic entomologists were few and far between, determination of the post-mortem interval was the domain of such an expert, not a forensic pathologist, however eminent.

CHAPTER 10

An Echo of Spilsburyism?

Echoes of the Past

Once Spilsbury had made up his mind, nothing could change it, including evidence to the contrary. His old adversary, Sydney Smith, came to the conclusion that once Spilsbury had given his opinion, he could not change it. Sadly, on occasion, not even evidence to the contrary could effect a change in the great man's evidence. Occasionally that proved to be a saving grace, but it could also produce major injustices. This aspect of Spilsburyism finds an echo in some of today's experts in many jurisdictions and also in those who inherited the baton from him and also from Smith. It occurred in what is now acknowledged to be one of the most notorious miscarriages of justice in British history—Timothy Evans. It was an injustice that could perhaps have been prevented if Donald Teare had avoided a mistake an expert of his ability should never have made.

Within three years of Spilsbury's suicide, murders at 10 Rillington Place hit the headlines for the first time. It would become a case that the three eminent pathologists, Francis Camps, Keith Simpson and Donald Teare would agree about, but eventually two senior judges would nevertheless agree that they were wrong about Timothy Evans—the first of four innocent men to hang in the 1950s.[1]

Inauspicious Beginnings

The opportunity to identify the donor of the semen found in murder victim, Beryl Evans, was lost permanently due to Teare's astonishing failure to take the swabs even though the bodies of Beryl and Geraldine Evans were subsequently exhumed. By then it had degenerated. Even in 1950 such a failure was extraordinary, especially as Teare's findings were that there may have been an attempt to sexually penetrate Beryl

1. George Kelly, Mahmood Mattan and Derek Bentley were the others.

after her death. While Teare may have assumed that the semen was not significant due to marital relations between Beryl and her husband, he should not have allowed an assumption to trump proof. That information was kept from the jury. Both Teare and Christie gave evidence for the prosecution. Evans was deprived of vital evidence. His case was that Christie, another tenant at the property, who was later exposed as one of Britain's most depraved serial killers, was the real murderer, but the investigation had been very shoddy.

At first there were few who championed the cause of 25-year-old Timothy Evans when it really mattered. There's no doubt that Evans' 19 year-old wife Beryl, and baby daughter, Geraldine, were murdered and that the star witness against Evans was later revealed to be the evil man that he really was, rather than the respectable man the jury that convicted Evans had believed him to be. John Reginald Halliday Christie was hanged in 1953 before the full extent of his involvement in the murders of Beryl and Geraldine could be established. It was, of course, obvious that Christie's despicable crimes would have to be investigated in order to establish whether a terrible miscarriage of justice had occurred, but thanks to a rush to the gallows with indecent haste, these investigations had to take place without the investigators having access to two vital players—the only ones who knew for certain what the truth was—Evans and Christie.

But there were obvious signs that a very serious injustice was unfolding, or at least there should have been. A human thigh bone in plain view in the garden was not observed by police. Evidence of Christie's crimes was present, but not searched for. During the Second World War Christie began his serial killing. There were other bodies in 10 Rillington Place—some had been there before Evans and his young family moved in. Christie's final three victims were Hectorina MacLennan, Kathleen Maloney and Rita Nelson. He had sexually assaulted them as well. They had been murdered between January and March 1953, about three years after Evans had been hanged. Their bodies had been left in the papered-over kitchen pantry next to the wash-house where the bodies of Beryl and Geraldine Evans had been left. The body of Christie's wife Ethel, who had defended him as 'a good man', when accused by Evans, was found under the floorboards of the living room in March 1953. She had been murdered in December 1952 and a further two, Ruth Fuerst and Muriel Eady in the garden — they had been murdered in the 1940s. Camps was the pathologist on the second occasion that 10 Rillington Place hit the headlines. Christie had killed eight people — all female — over almost a decade. If the jury trying Timothy Evans had known in 1950 that far from being the respectable man he pretended to be, Christie was a depraved serial killer who had killed before, and done so using the same method, it is inconceivable that they would have convicted Evans.

CHAPTER 11

The Swansong of the Three Musketeers

Crimes and Misdemeanours

Donald Teare had been the pathologist when 10 Rillington Place first came to public attention. Timothy Evans' account seemed far-fetched at first glance, but time would vindicate him—sadly far too late. Evans undoubtedly misled police and confessed before retracting it and accusing the seemingly respectable tenant, Christie. As he faced the gallows Evans could not have known the true character of Christie, or that his seemingly preposterous story would be proved true. Evans had accused the star witness of killing his wife in exactly the manner that Christie had used previously and would use again. Evans did not have the intelligence to invent such a story. It was an egregious miscarriage of justice and one that could have been avoided if the investigation had been thorough. Police missed vital evidence that would have exposed Christie's previous crimes, the murders of Ruth Fuerst in August 1943 and Muriel Eady in October 1944 if their search of 10 Rillington Place had been competent.

It would prove not to be the only thing that was below par in this inquiry. Teare made the inexplicable error of failing to test for semen, despite compelling evidence that it needed to be done. The bruising of Beryl Evans' vagina indicated the possibility, likelihood even, of rape, but Teare's error would have dire consequences. He would get a chance to put right this error. Just over three years after Christie helped to send Evans to the gallows, the depth of Christie's depravity was exposed. Ironically, the serial killer's racism contributed to his downfall. He and his wife Ethel objected to West Indian immigrants moving in to 10 Rillington Place. The Christies saw themselves as superior to their new neighbours and that contributed to Christie's decision to move on—astonishingly he decided to move after he murdered Ethel and left her remains there. His neighbours discovered the bodies hidden in the alcove. Christie was soon the subject of a manhunt that ended in his arrest and subsequent execution.

The Inauspicious Swansong of the Three Musketeers

Forensic pathology provided little that could conclusively prove which one of Evans or Christie had killed Beryl and Geraldine Evans. Trophies in the form of pubic hairs were mentioned by Professor Simpson in his book *40 Years of Murder.* Christie lived there too and had access to various places in the house. He collected them, but how could he possibly explain taking and keeping the pubic hairs of Evans' wife? There were problems within the Evans' marriage. The exhumation provided no evidence of sexual activity on Beryl Evans, but it had been done years later and after Teare had inexplicably failed to take swabs from the vagina at the time despite him observing bruising to it, but what did the forensic science prove? Sadly not much. Its potential was ruined by Teare's inexplicable error. It is impossible to say who the donor would have been proved to be in terms of forensic science then available. However, it could have been resolved even now through DNA testing if original material of sufficient quality remained to be tested. This is another reason to ensure that correct procedures must be adhered to.

Once it became clear that Christie must have been a killer regardless of the deaths of Beryl and Geraldine Evans, exhumations were ordered, partly to try to resolve the semen issue. The Three Musketeers were summoned. Camps made it very clear to Simpson and Teare that he was in charge. All three of them agreed their findings. Simpson described the findings as disappointing as they failed to resolve the main issues, but he raised another — that of Christie's predilection for collecting pubic hairs of his victims as trophies. The obvious point being that Beryl Evans' pubic hairs were intact, so why if Christie had murdered her had he not taken his usual trophy? First of all, how could he explain that to Evans — something that would have been obvious during the investigation and trial that followed? How could he blame Evans for the murder if such a trophy, which Evans had no interest in or inclination to take, had been taken? What possible reason could Evans have for taking such a trophy from his wife? Christie would surely have known that. He had not evaded capture for a decade without cunning. Christie was many things, but fool was not one of them.

CHAPTER 12

Obfuscation

Lies, Damned Lies and Official Reports

The discovery that Christie was a vicious and depraved serial killer, rather than the respectable man he was portrayed to be, meant that there would have to be enquiries into Evans' conviction.[1] Christie's case was far less complex or controversial. There was no doubt about his guilt. The only issue at his trial was his sanity. The pathology evidence was straight forward, or relatively so, but Camps would not have the opportunity that was presented to Teare. The remains that he examined did not have the recent sexual activity that had so affected the inquiry into the murder of Beryl Evans. Christie's character had undergone a 180° sea change. It was now in his interests to portray himself as deranged, but even in his self-serving interviews, there were limits. He was prepared to own up to murdering Beryl Evans, but not the baby Geraldine. He claimed that Beryl's death was an accident—a back-street abortion that went wrong. This was also the story that Evans claimed Christie had told him regarding Beryl's death. Evans also claimed that Christie told him that he—Evans—would be blamed for Beryl's death, so he should leave. Evans did after being assured that Geraldine was safe. How could taking a trophy of Beryl's pubic hairs be explained in this scenario of Beryl's death? Plainly, it could not. Does this explain why Christie controlled his bestial urges at least in that respect in this murder? While Evans could be deceived—perhaps easily—what about the police and lawyers? The question of whose semen had been deposited in Beryl remained moot. If it had been identified as Christie's, the game would have been up, but thanks to Teare's incredible error, that could not be proved.

1. At the time defendants tended to be charged with just one of the murders, even if they were suspected of having committed more. That was the case with Evans and it provided a way out for a system anxious to deny the extent that it had wronged a vulnerable young man.

Christie's only hope of avoiding the gallows was the insanity plea, but the jury rejected it. His appeal was swiftly rejected. There was no hope of mercy being recommended by the Home Secretary, Sir David Maxwell-Fyfe. Christie was hanged on July 15th 1953 — just over 15 weeks after he was arrested, but the controversy refused to die with him. There were official reports, notably those of John Scott-Henderson QC and Mr Justice (Sir Daniel) Brabin and even exhumations, but the controversy stubbornly refused to be laid to rest. Brabin's report concluded that it was more probable than not that Evans had murdered his wife, but not his daughter — a finding that finds little favour now. It should be remembered that Evans was never charged with Beryl's murder — it was normal practice to charge defendants with just one. This resulted in the opportunity to suggest that there may have been no miscarriage of justice. The Crown had simply hanged Timothy Evans for the wrong murder. In other words, no foul, but the system was so fair that it gave a probably guilty man a pardon anyway.

Occam's Razor

This should not have been tolerated. Teare had been the original pathologist, but had made an incredible error for an expert of his standing. Despite bruising in Beryl Evans' vagina, Teare failed to take swabs for semen. Had this been done, as it plainly should have been, the question of whether Christie had tried to force his attentions onto Mrs Evans could have been resolved and with that powerful scientific evidence could possibly have been obtained as well. It is impossible to know if semen was deposited in Beryl Evans now and if it had been, who had deposited it. Teare's error prevented that from happening when it could have made all the difference. It is an astonishing oversight for such a renowned expert and one that has left a shadow of doubt where certainty was possible. The consequences of this error were never addressed by the various reports.

The exposure of Christie as a sadistic serial killer had an immediate and obvious effect. The Home Secretary at the time ordered the then Recorder of Portsmouth to conduct a review. Among the people that John Scott-Henderson QC interviewed was Christie. He concluded that Christie's confession to murdering Beryl was in fact a cunning plan to bolster his insanity defence—the more the merrier—but Scott-Henderson fails to explain why Christie would not then admit to murdering the baby Geraldine too if that was the case. After all, murdering a defenceless baby was as insane as it could get. The post-mortem examinations failed to resolve the issues, but Scott-Henderson concluded that Evans was guilty of the murders of Beryl and Geraldine Evans, meaning that he believed that there were two killers who murdered in exactly the same fashion at the same time and place, acting independently of each other without knowing that the other was an active killer, rather than the far more likely conclusion that there was just one killer and that man was Christie—Occam's Razor.

CHAPTER 13

Posterity's Verdict

The Final Judgement

Posterity proved kinder to Timothy Evans than his contemporaries and the eminent forensic pathologists, Camps, Simpson and Teare, had been. Evans was posthumously pardoned in 1966, but the nature of his trial and conviction had left the door open to do so in a manner that disputed his innocence. Despite there being no doubt in the 1950s that both Beryl and Geraldine had been murdered by the same man, Sir Daniel Brabin's report suggested otherwise, meaning that it was possible for those wanting to claim that Evans was not an innocent man to do so without the inconvenience of actually trying him for that crime — Beryl's murder. It gave the authorities the opportunity to claim that Evans had simply been hanged for the wrong crime, but that the system was so fair that it had pardoned him anyway. However, this was a miscarriage of justice that refused to be buried.

Almost 40 years after the pardon and over half a century too late for Evans, his case finally reached the courts again. "I am happy to express my agreement with the conclusion of the [Criminal Cases Review] Commission that Timothy Evans has been exonerated of the murders of his wife and child", Lord Justice (Sir Stanley) Burnton said in a judicial review of the Commission's decision not to refer the case back for appeal in 2004. The judicial review had been brought by members of Evans' family because technically Evans remains convicted of the crime that he was hanged for — the 'pardon' never quashed the conviction.[1]

1. Six years before, Lord Justice (Sir Christopher) Rose read the judgement quashing the conviction of the wrongfully convicted and hanged Mahmood Mattan. The Court of Appeal therefore has the jurisdiction and power to quash the conviction of a wrongfully executed person. The comments made by Burnton clearly establish that there is at the very least a realistic prospect of the conviction being quashed if it was referred back for appeal. The convictions of Derek Bentley and George Kelly — also wrongly convicted and hanged in the 1950s — were quashed by the Court of Appeal after Mattan's case. Ironically, Evans remains the only one of those cases whose conviction remains intact — free pardon or not. Burnton's comments aside, it remains a miscarriage of justice for an unsustainable conviction to remain on the record in any form whatsoever.

Vindicated

"It is recognised that he committed neither murder", Burnton continued. "The free pardon which he was granted was a formal vindication and when granted the only available vindication of the only murder of which he had been convicted. The Home Secretary did all he could. The subsequent payment of compensation to his surviving family assessed on the basis that he was wholly innocent makes the position abundantly clear. I hope that these public expressions in open court of his innocence will give some solace to his family".

This makes it clear that the conclusions of Teare in particular no longer found favour. And this was not the only miscarriage of justice that Teare had made a serious error in. Although Teare was on the defence's side in the Maxwell Confait Inquiry along with Simpson, they both made a terrible error regarding the timing of Confait's death—one that experienced pathologists like them should never have made, even though the performance of the Crown's expert, Professor James Cameron, was far worse than their's. Like Spilsbury before them, this happened before Michael Heath, Paula Lannas, Freddy Patel and Peter Acland supposedly pierced the aura of expert forensic pathologists once and for all.

CHAPTER 14

Not its Finest Hour

Travesties

Sir Bernard Spilsbury was long dead; competitive tendencies had seen the Three Musketeers go their separate ways and Michael Heath was not even qualified when a shameful miscarriage of justice that would change the face of British justice occurred. Strangely, in the annals of miscarriages of justice work, this case is denied its deserved place as one of Britain's most important. It is a case that made history several times — the Maxwell Confait Inquiry. It was far from forensic pathology's finest hour. The errors, especially those of the late Professor James Cameron, were crass, to put it mildly, even for over 40 years ago.

Cameron also contributed to one of Australia's most notorious miscarriages of justice — the tragic death of two-months-old baby Azaria Chamberlain. On August 17th 1980, Azaria was taken from Uluru — formerly known as Ayer's Rock in Australia's Northern Territory — by a dingo. Her body was never recovered. An appalling miscarriage of justice followed, which despite the quashing of convictions of her parents, Lindy and Michael Chamberlain, eight years after her death, took 32 years to fully put right.[1] Professor Cameron's evidence had played a vital part in bringing them to trial. Cameron said that he had discovered an incised wound around the neck of Azaria's jumpsuit,

1. Azaria's parents were wrongfully convicted in October 1982 — Lindy of murder and Michael of being an accessory after the fact. In 1986 the case against them was seriously undermined by the chance discovery of the baby's missing matinée jacket, as police searched for bones of tourist, David Brett, that may have been carried off by dingoes, after he had fallen to his death in an area of Uluru, which had several lairs occupied by dingoes. This was compelling evidence that the Chamberlains had told the truth all along. Azaria had been attacked and taken by a dingo just as her parents had said. Their convictions were quashed on appeal in September 1988.

   An inquest in 1995 reached an open verdict, which proved unsatisfactory. Another inquest in June 2012 concluded that the cause of Azaria's death was the result of being attacked and taken by a dingo. Her death certificate was amended accordingly. The scientific evidence at the Chamberlains' trial, including the erroneous conclusions drawn by Professor Cameron had finally been thoroughly discredited. Strangely, Cameron's awful performance in the Maxwell Confait Inquiry failed to impact upon his credibility in the Azaria Chamberlain Inquiry.

along with the imprint of an adult's hand on it too. Cameron claimed this was clearly visible on photographs. That evidence helped to get her parents—they have since divorced—charged. It strongly implied that Azaria's throat had been cut. However, the prosecution's case was subsequently discredited, as evidence emerged proving that Azaria had indeed been taken by a dingo as the Chamberlains had insisted all along.

Shameful Failings

A year before the Chamberlains were convicted, the Royal Commission on Criminal Procedures, chaired by Professor Sir Cyril Philips, ended. It had been necessitated by the shameful miscarriage of justice suffered by the Catford Three in the Maxwell Confait Inquiry. Cameron had made a complete hash of the forensic pathology in that case. In the early hours of April 22nd 1972, a fire was put out at Confait's digs in Catford, South-East London. A young man's body was discovered and autopsied by Cameron. Initially, Cameron gave a range for the time of death, which was the basis for the defence lawyers to prepare their clients' alibi evidence for trial, but during his evidence at the trial Cameron shifted his opinion, saying that death could have occurred as recently as half an hour before the fire. His changing of the time of death caused serious problems for the defence, especially of the vulnerable 18 year-old Colin Lattimore. It was an ambush that should have resulted in censure and a mistrial. The prosecution needed Cameron's change of opinion as Lattimore's alibi for the original timing was strong, but there were other reasons for the change too. The previous opinion given by Cameron meant that the killers must have committed the murder and then stayed around to set a fire, hours later. It was an absurd case-scenario, but one that failed to register as such with police or prosecutors. It is very unlikely that the forensic pathology would have gone so badly wrong in that case if the changes that Mick Burdiss, Gary Pugh and Barclay helped to establish in 2004 (see **Part Three—Peers**) had been in place at the time.

Eventually, the whole case unravelled. The fire had nothing to do with Maxwell Confait's murder. The esteemed forensic pathologists Donald Teare and Keith Simpson challenged Cameron's view regarding the time of death, which was later proved to be hopelessly wrong. They had said that Confait could not have died later than 10.30 in the night of April 21st. Their opinions resulted in a successful appeal, but while it was true that the fire could not have been later than 10.30 pm on April 21st, it was also wildly inaccurate, as the sadly deceased Professors Alan Usher and Keith Mant proved.[2] Discolouration of the organs showed that rigor mortis was not in its initial stages; it was on the verge of passing. Confait had been dead for at least two days. Three eminent forensic pathologists had made a mistake that none of them, let alone all three, should have made. This was, on any view, an abysmal failure of forensic pathology — one that would surely lead to serious repercussions, especially for Cameron, but also for the science.

Sadly, it failed to have that impact on both counts. Cameron, Teare and Simpson gave way to the next generation — Camps was already dead by then. He would probably have relished the embarrassment the Confait case had caused to the other two Musketeers. It soon emerged — or should have done — that hubris had been passed on to the next generation too. Michael Heath, Paula Lannas, Freddy Patel and Peter Acland would at least pay some price for their shoddy work and professional arrogance, as they would lose their status as Home Office pathologists. All four would be removed from the Register of Home Office Pathologists — Patel would be struck off by the General Medical Council (GMC).

2. Professor Mant died in 2000 and Usher two years earlier. Both did not live to see the changes in forensic pathology brought in by Barclay, Burdiss and Pugh.

PART THREE

PEERS

"Our lives begin to end the day we become silent about things that matter".

Dr Martin Luther King Jnr.

CHAPTER 15

Competing Interests

Primacy

Spilsburyism had survived Sir Bernard—it proved to be a pervasive problem that took decades to overcome. Pathologists, especially those of his ilk, believed that they had a God-given right to authority. They had resisted change for years and in some cases it had led to disastrous errors, such as those of Donald Teare in the Timothy Evans case, and also Teare, Simpson and Cameron in the Maxwell Confait Inquiry. As forensic sciences developed, new problems emerged, or even new manifestations of old ones.

As the Schiedammer Park crimes approached correct resolution, Britain tackled the legacy of Spilsburyism. The Dutch DNA expert Richard Eikelenboom explains that competition between experts almost had dire consequences in the Schiedammer Park crimes. Eikelenboom developed the protocols to obtain Low Template DNA in that case. It was extraordinarily sensitive—obtainable from a single cell. That meant contamination was a real risk. The protocols used minimised that risk, but nothing could prevent the problems caused by shoddy procedures, especially in other disciplines. The Schiedammer Park Inquiry was botched on several levels. It was solvable in part because of Eikelenboom's work. DNA offered the best chance of correctly resolving the crimes, but it was almost wrecked due to shockingly lax procedures.

Crass Procedures

Ten-year-old Nienke Kleiss had fought hard for her life. Sadly, she could not fight off Wik Haalmeijer. However, she gave scientists and investigators the evidence that they needed to catch the perpetrator, but her efforts were almost sabotaged by incredibly inappropriate procedures which contaminated and destroyed evidence. "In Holland it is more or less getting better now, but at that time we were still fighting over the politics of homicide cases", Eikelenboom explained. "The problem with her DNA was that the front side of her body was completely covered with mucus from the bronchia, because she was strangled. You know if you strangle someone you get a lot of fluid from the lungs and that was completely moved in the body-bag. The body was still warm with loads of DNA from the victim".

The error that was made in this case was mind-boggling. "I was setting up how to get this [trace DNA from small amounts] in '99", he explains. "There was no way that the police always put the scientist on the scene, because I was the only one going there. At that stage there was not a team. They could call me 24 hours, but they get into a lot of trouble because they remove the body within half an hour, all because they were thinking that it was getting dark or raining or something, so what they did was put the body in the body-bag, but of course we now know that this was wrong, but you have to look at it in that time. It was common for bodies to go into body-bags, but of course trace coverings was not to go into body-bags and still they don't do that, but of course it's high profile. What happens is that we find a lot of blood on the backside of the victim and this blood appears to be of Maikel. The pathologist says 'keep the body as you find it', but they didn't. There were some lesions on the neck, but also with the shoe, so now the whole shoe and the neck are covered in blood".

That caused serious problems which should have been avoided. Potentially vital evidence that the shoe would have held—the lace had been taken from it, possibly by the killer—had been hopelessly compromised, ironically in an effort to preserve evidence.

Wasted Evidence

"She was found like this and she goes into the body-bag like this, but they probably did put the shoe in the body-bag and pulled her over the blood of Maikel", Eikelenboom said. "That's the only explanation I can think of".

And that was that. Shockingly lax procedures had allowed potentially vital evidence to be lost for ever. This happened in a case where 'touch DNA' was going to be important. Nevertheless, useful evidence was still obtained. Eikelenboom explains the other problems. Evidence was obtained against the odds, only for its significance to be concealed.

"No scientist ever likes DNA mixture from three persons, but in this case it was inevitable that we had to look for that", Eikelenboom said, explaining the further problems that had to be considered in this case. "[O]ther problems, with blood and bronchial fluids from the victim, was very likely and, then, skin (epithelial) cells coming from the hand of the perpetrator too. You know [the chances are] 85% of getting profile from blood or fluid and only 16% chance of getting epithelial cells".

He explains the significance of this. "If you want my DNA more force has to be applied. It's not very logical to get DNA if I just touch the place, if you find anything at all. I did 100 cases in 2000 of contact DNA. Only 20% you get a profile, which means you don't in 80%, so even though you know someone was strangled like that, you hardly lose any material from your hand if you commit a crime. Blood, saliva or semen is very easy, but contact DNA is very difficult and that's what is going to get us Low Copy Number DNA. This is the first case in Holland where we use LCN DNA".

Despite the terrible error made by Dutch investigators, the rape and murder of Nienke Kleiss and attempted murder of eleven-year-old Maikel Willebrand were eventually solved.[1]

1. The inquiry into the Schiedammer Park crimes was terribly botched. Willebrand survived by playing dead. After Haalmeijer had left the park Willebrand stopped a passing cyclist and asked him to call the police. Kees Borsboom did that. Borsboom was subsequently wrongly convicted. The case was only resolved correctly because Haalmeijer was later arrested for two unrelated rapes and insisted on DNA testing to corroborate his unsolicited confession to the Schiedammer Park crimes.

CHAPTER 16

An Independent Expert's View

The Dangers of Status

In homicide cases the forensic pathologist will usually be the first forensic scientist to perform scientific examinations. They will generally take samples from the body. Consequently, the integrity and competence of forensic pathologists can also affect the ability of other experts to obtain and interpret scientific evidence. Sir Bernard Spilsbury and his contemporaries helped to bring the profession respectability. Spilsbury had an aura that allowed his opinions, which had on occasion transcended the boundaries of the science to impress judges and juries, even when challenged. Inevitably, that led to injustices. His hubris often went unchallenged, and even when challenged, it often made no difference, despite lives being at stake.

The problems of Spilsburyism had permeated the second generation and found their way into the next one too. It would not be the last in Britain where pre-eminence and prima donnas held sway over forensic pathology. These were problems not restricted to Britain alone and not even to forensic pathology. Spilsbury's success was itself very dangerous, as his status stood above the profession and even the science itself.

"He was the leading pathologist for 20 or 30 years and there was a cult in that time", said Professor Dave Barclay, the former Head of Physical Evidence at the National Crimes and Operations Faculty (NCOF). "The traditional joke, 'What's the difference between God and a pathologist? God doesn't think he's a pathologist' originated at that time and it applied until fairly recently, so there is always a danger when one person becomes the pre-eminent expert".

Status

There were no processes to curb the arrogance that came with Spilsbury's pre-eminent status, bar the hit or miss trial process and even that was tainted by summing-ups that bordered on the adulation of a hero by a fan.[1] How could a jury not be influenced by such a recommendation from the judge? And that was in a case where there were plenty of credible experts opposing him. It mattered nought — Norman Thorne was convicted and hanged for murder despite the serious scientific doubts about Spilsbury's evidence.

Despite the occasional challenge to his status by scientists whom history has subsequently vindicated, the appearance of Spilsbury usually meant doom for the opposing side and he revelled in that status. "Spilsbury and other forensic scientists — in those days there weren't that many — and because they were the pre-eminent experts, they weren't challenged", Barclay said.

There were further problems too. On rare occasions, Spilsbury was properly challenged, but juries and judges were spell-bound by the undisputed star of the profession. "Other experts, even when they did challenge him, the jury could say, 'Well it's Spilsbury; he must be right', and that wasn't always the case", Barclay said. The dangers of over-reliance on Spilsbury were clear and there were no preventative means to hold Spilsbury accountable during his lifetime. He made his science understandable to them and so they were more receptive to his opinions, scientific or not. Prosecutors loved him — he got results — but when they had defence briefs, not so much.

Flawed

I think he wasn't as scientifically neutral as he should have been", Barclay said of Spilsbury. "Nowadays we're taught to use Bayesian statistics when we're assessing significance, but more importantly, to use Bayesian thinking all the time. Bayesian thinking says, 'Look I've got this nice observation. How likely is it that I could get this observation from any other cause'? I think that's the thing that Spilsbury didn't do. As soon as you start thinking like that, you're inevitably assessing the significance of your results. Yeah, I could get that little mark in Crippen's — well Belle's

1. See Chapter 3 **The Martyr to Spilsburyism** in our forthcoming book **Forensic Pathology — Righting Wrongs**. The judge, Sir William Finlay, described Spilsbury as "the greatest living pathologist".

tummy[2]—but could it have come from a number of different causes? It might not be a scar. It might be a fold of skin. It might be an artefact and he didn't think like that. He identified it as what he said it was and then it became 100%".

Arrogance in experts and over-reliance upon them, especially any who achieve pre-eminent status like Spilsbury was a constant danger, but the pervasive or even corrosive influence of Spilsburyism was not confined to his approach to the science. Hubris over opinions was far from confined to Spilsbury. Eventually solutions to those problems emerged, but other aspects still permeate the criminal justice system—an inevitable consequence of the adversarial system of justice. "There's a basic flaw in the CPS system that the more definite the opinions that somebody gives the better the CPS like them, so they use them again and so on and the whole thing carries on until somebody comes a cropper, so that's a very poor system", Barclay says. "It also applied in 2004–05 to a couple of specialist experts, because there was nobody to peer-review their work—nobody to check their work".

He explains his preference. "I would rather it was a system whereby everybody was peer-reviewed as part of a proper scientific institution—not working individually as a sort of cottage industry", he said.

This is what now happens in forensic pathology, but as we have seen, the baton was passed and there were still problems, even though none of the three Musketeers achieved Spilsbury's pre-eminent status. Trial processes and inquests alone could not curb the errors even when they opposed each other and once the baton was passed on again to Heath et al, even worse problems emerged—ones that finally brought an end to the dominance of forensic pathologists.

2. Belle Elmore was the stage name of Crippen's wife Cora—whose partial remains Spilsbury was alleged to have identified by the supposed 'scar' on the skin.

CHAPTER 17

Perceptions

DNA

There is a perception, in the public at least, that forensic science is DNA first, second, third, fourth and fifth, and other sciences, maybe later. So, how does someone at the cutting edge of forensic science view this perception, and the use of other sciences being involved in the use of forensic science, both in terms of proving innocence and implicating people as well? Professor Dave Barclay has an important perspective on this as he has conducted numerous reviews both during his work at the National Crime Faculty and subsequently.

"Well that's a fallacious argument anyway, because even in the UK, you cannot use DNA on its own", Barclay explains. "You need some other piece of evidence, but *forensic science is about results in context.* Exactly the same result will mean something completely different if you change the context — the circumstances — so you need to re-establish that context and often the pathology, physical evidence, fingerprints will be part of that context in which DNA sits anyway. And in many, many cases of sexual assault or rape, the DNA is almost irrelevant. If it's an alleged stranger-rape, fine, that might help you to identify the person, but if it's not, the issue will be one of consent and everything else to do with forensic science will help you over that issue. Say it is a rape case and the issue is one of consent, it will be everything else that happened — where she was attacked, if she says she saw the offender take some cocaine, does he have cocaine in him? The offender went into the bathroom; are his finger-marks in the bathroom and so on? So it's everything else; *so it's nonsense that DNA is the main thing.* The advantage of DNA and fingerprints are they're the best two methods of identifying an *unknown* person directly and of course they're both equally good at doing that. Some people say that DNA is actually cheaper than fingerprinting" [my emphasis].

Importance

Of course, DNA is very important, but it requires valid procedures that can identify where to look for significant DNA that can solve the relevant problems, such as what would have been shed by the perpetrator in the course of committing the crime, or equally important what would have been shed by the victim in the course of the crime committed that could identify the perpetrator. In many cases both can be obtained and that will constitute powerful evidence, but the very power of DNA—its great power of discrimination (eliminating people and narrowing down people of interest) and its sensitivity (DNA can be obtained from a single cell and be easily amplified) makes contamination a major risk. That emphasises the importance of stringent procedures. An example of the dangers and problems caused by poor practice was given by Richard Eikelenboom in the previous chapter, which leads on to the core question, what is the function of forensic science?

"Well it should be and *is* the function of forensic science to help prove innocence because when your stuff comes in the lab, you're completely neutral and impartial and one thing that's often forgotten is that forensic science is a hell of a lot better at eliminating things than associating things" [his emphasis], Professor Barclay explains. "If you find two things are associated, whether it's fibres or fluff from carpet or whatever, you have to assess the significance of that link, that positive link, but if you find something that does not match—if you get a DNA profile from somebody and it does not match, you can absolutely eliminate that suspect, so forensic science is always better at eliminating than associating. That's something I would say of maybe every hundred items that's seized at the crime-scene, maybe ten percent or 20 percent are sent to the lab, maybe 20 percent of those are examined and 20 percent of those are actually given in evidence. As soon as you get one of those things that shows that something didn't happen or that exculpates the person, then that's the end of it. You don't go on to do all the rest of the tests. You only really go on to assess the significance of things if you get inculpatory evidence".

CHAPTER 18

Regulation

The Other FSS

The Forensic Science Regulator was established in June 2007. Andrew Rennison — a former police officer — was the Regulator from 2008 until he stepped down in August 2014.[1] "I have no power to review individual cases and that's not the remit given to me by Ministers", Rennison said. "My remit is to look at the quality standards of forensic science. I can and I am asked by Ministers to manage complaints around the quality of science, so if there is a miscarriage of justice and there is a complaint about the quality of the science involved, then I'll look at the science generically across a range of cases, not a particular case".

Rennison is quick to point out that things had moved on since the bad old days of unregulated forensic science. He credits the now defunct Forensic Science Service with leading the way. "We're in a very different world now", he said. "The forensic science laboratories in the UK have all adopted an international standard for testing calibration laboratories. This standard was first introduced in 1995. The Forensic Science Service, which was then the leading laboratory in the UK, led the way towards the adoption of this standard. The standard is ISO 17025. ISO being International Standards Organisation".

Standards and Accreditation

This standard is applied as follows. "It's an international standard for testing calibration laboratories, which is built on three corner-stones: 1) an independent assessment of the robustness of the management systems of the laboratory, including the core management systems; 2) it assesses the competence of the scientists and equally importantly, in

1. Rennison was appointed a Commissioner of the CCRC in November 2013, but his term did not start until he stepped down as Forensic Science Regulator and also CCTV Commissioner. Rennison gave two exclusive interviews to **The Fitted-In Project**. Rennison was succeeded by Dr Gillian Tully for three years, and reappointed for a further three years in November 2017.

fact probably most importantly, it demands clear evidence of the validation of the methods employed, so if you are a DNA laboratory, you will apply for accreditation against ISO 17025 for the DNA methods you are employing", Rennison explains. "You are assessed by the United Kingdom Accreditation Service [UKAS], who will employ, as they need them, DNA technical experts—I know a number of these people who go out and do these visits. They will come and visit your laboratory and they will take you through a very robust assessment regime, which will include assessment of your training records for your staff. They will interview staff. They will observe staff undertaking their work. They will audit the results of that work and they'll demand to see clear evidence that you have validated your methods through validation reports, etc. and if they are satisfied as an independent audit function that you meet those three corner-stones, they will award you accreditation against this standard for the scope of work you have applied for. You can log onto the United Kingdom Accreditation Service website search LGC Forensics [for example] and you will see a list of all their laboratories and for each laboratory there will be an accreditation certificate that shows you what methods they're accredited for in accordance with ISO 17025. They have a public register of all the companies they accredit. There's a range of forensic science providers there. That standard's been in place for laboratories, or implemented since 1995, so now all across the UK all commercial laboratories work to this standard".

However, these standards are not limited to Britain. They inspired a global standard. "The accreditation bodies around the world have formed an organisation called the International Laboratory Accreditation Corporation, referred to as ILAC. ILAC have taken ISO 17025 and have published a supplementary document referred to as ILAC G19, which again is available on ILAC's website. There's no copyright issues on G19 and G19 is published as a means of contextualising ISO 17025 for the forensic laboratories and it enhances various aspects of it. I have looked at all of that as the basis of the quality standards framework for the UK and I published back in July this year Codes of Practice and conduct for the providers of forensic science services for the criminal justice system using ISO 17025 as the base standard system, but enhancing it even further for the UK context. It is well worth looking at the UK's use of DNA technology as an example of how that standard's framework can work very effectively, because this standard came into being in 1995, so post-dating the offence in the Lynette White Inquiry, which means that the forensic science providers had to take a much, much more robust approach to the science they deliver, so if they are bringing particular methods in, they've got to be valid, fit for purpose and tested, which wasn't in place in the late 80s".

These standards, if they had been applied in time to forensic pathology, could have prevented at least some of the mayhem caused by Acland, Heath, Lannas and Patel. So, why wasn't it applied? And secondly, what role should the Forensic Science Regulator have had in regulating forensic pathology, and what powers should he or she have?

CHAPTER 19

Application

Accountability

As the then Forensic Science Regulator, Andrew Rennison, made clear, the standard was there to govern the provision of forensic science since 1995 at the least. He published Codes of Practice and conduct for the providers of forensic science services for the criminal justice system using ISO 17025 as the base standard system, but enhancing it even further for the UK. His Codes were binding more recently, but ISO 17025 has been an enforceable standard since 1995. So how would it work in practice with disputes over what could or should have been done?

"Well it will never deal with a difference of opinion", Rennison explained. "You're always going to have to trust the judgement of the experts in the day, but what you have behind that now are far more robust validation processes and standards they have to work to, so they're far more accountable now than they ever were".

But does the Regulator have sufficient powers to deliver that accountability?

"Well, you were at the starting point of changes in 1995, so it's taken a number of years for the standards to creep through the laboratories", Rennison said. "It only kicked off in '95, so the point I'm trying to make is the changes were made in '95. Since '95 a whole new quality standards framework is in place, though I have to say you still have to rely on the judgement of experts and there's always going to be arguments around that and we have it even nowadays. That's what court trials are for. Court trials are invariably resolving the differences between experts in evidence and there's no standard you can ever create that will carve its way through that. What you do demand is that when experts give evidence that they are using evidence that is robust. It's tested. It's valid, peer-reviewed and they've got to be prepared, more so than they were in 1995".

However, this did not apply to pathology. Despite the obligations of ISO 17025 and the need to peer-review, it was not mandatory in that forensic science for almost a decade and some pathologists quit the Home Office system rather than submit to the changes implemented in the mid-2000s by the Home Office. What does that say about the quality of their work previously?

A New Era

It is, of course, clear that forensic science and the delivery of it by providers has improved greatly. Resolution is possible now, according to Rennison. "It's helped by the commercialisation of the market, because you're not reliant on one service provider to provide expert opinion", he says. "The police do it quite routinely now. If they receive an opinion from one provider, they then have the ability to go elsewhere, so you could ask the same question of a different provider, which is exactly what the Met Police did in the Rachel Nickell case. They weren't happy with the advice they got from one provider, so they went elsewhere, which solved the case, so now actually you've got a broader range of expertise to draw upon, which is a positive in the system . The monopoly with the FSS came with some real advantages, but it came with some disadvantages and one of those was you were actually limited in expert advice, so I think if you want to look at historically back in '95, and I know there were quite heated discussions about the appropriate method to use, the police nowadays could draw on alternative experts and ask: 'what do you think'? And we see that happen and it works very well".

However, this does nothing to redress the errors of the past? "If I had been in existence then and there was very heated debate about particular methodology we might have been able to step in and look at the validity of the science behind it", Rennison said. "We don't step in and look at individual cases. That is not my role. There is me and me alone. I spread myself thin enough as it is, so we do not get involved in individual cases. We cannot. We have no power to. If people refer issues to us we will look at it and we will advise where we can under our complaints procedure and it's never happened yet. I've never had individual cases referred to me, but we do have the science referred to us".

This suggests that there is and was a mechanism to investigate and resolve examples of poor forensic science that has yet to be utilised. It begs the question, why has this not been used?

CHAPTER 20

Regulatory Powers

Individual Cases

The Forensic Science Regulator (FSR) has powers determined by Ministers. The FSR was established in 2008 without the powers to investigate individual cases, although general forensic science issues can be reviewed and regulated.

"I never comment on individuals", Rennison said. "I comment on the overall way that the science works and I'm glad to say, there's a whole new framework now and I'm pushing even further. I'm also glad that we have a broader expertise through the different organisations to draw upon, and also actually, forensic science nowadays is harmonising globally. So, actually there are now more harmonised opinions around the world to draw upon. For example, I am about to publish some new standards and guidelines around the interpretation of DNA profiles and we've been able to achieve consensus through colleagues in America, New Zealand and across Europe in doing that, so when we publish it, it will be a standard for the UK. But it's been peer-reviewed around the world and that's a very good example of how science now is so globalised. We need to draw upon that global expertise to raise standards, and it's working".

So what about redressing previous cases, or the science used in cases? Rennison says that is not the role of the FSR—just looking at the science and its validity. So, what role should the FSR have in the governance of forensic science?

Precedent

Professor Barclay suggests powers and a role for the FSR. "Well I think he has a role about governance as it is, but I think it should almost be like—I was going to say the Financial Services Authority,[1] but they're

1. The Financial Services Authority is now known as the Financial Conduct Authority.

not a good example to use", he said. "He should have teeth. I don't think forensic scientists deliberately make mistakes, or fiddle evidence, but I would say that wouldn't I? I have been a forensic scientist for 35 years, but when they do, or if there are failings in their processes which lead mistakes to go through the system, then I think something serious needs to be done about it to rectify the systems. *It's not just a question of a mistake being made, but whether there are systems in place to prevent them getting through.* And I would like the Forensic Science Regulator to have those powers to suspend people from doing casework or to stop them doing casework completely and there have been instances in the past where the Forensic Science Service, as it then was part of the Home Office, voluntarily did that. Dr [Alan] Clift's case is a good example. Dr Clift was working at the Birmingham laboratory at the time and gave evidence in the trial of a lorry driver who was charged with murder [John Preece] and he gave evidence that blood in the cab of the lorry was the same blood groups as the victim, which was quite powerful evidence and I think that Preece was eventually convicted. It later emerged that Preece had exactly the same blood groups and that Clift knew that. If you are a lorry driver, it's quite likely that you would cut yourself and leave blood in the cab and so on. This was pre-DNA" [my emphasis].

Role

This case illustrated the problems with regulatory powers. This was illustrated by the victim-blaming that Clift and his supporters attempted to justify his conduct.

"It was the late 1970s", Barclay said. "Clift and his supporters said, 'Well he wasn't asked the right questions by the defence, so it was the defence's fault.' The vast majority of forensic scientists including myself completely disagreed with that. I always thought that you had to give everything that you knew about the case when you were giving your evidence in chief. You don't wait for the defence to ask you the right questions if you think there's a deficiency or another explanation. I prefer to give that explanation in chief whether or not the prosecution barrister wanted me to and there were occasions where they definitely didn't want me to. I once refused to leave the witness box when instructed to by the judge, because I knew that something I said and the defence hadn't picked up on had left a misleading impression with the jury. Most other forensic scientists will have had similar experiences".

Professor Barclay believes that the highest standards should be demanded and that in general forensic scientists have those standards and want to be held to them. As in the old adage if you have nothing to hide, you have nothing to fear from stringent standards that demand the highest quality.

"I think every forensic scientist feels like that, or should, and if they don't, then the Forensic Regulator should take a very firm view of this sort of thing", Barclay said. "It's even more important now when we have lots of forensic providers. We used to have a very strong quality control organisation in the Forensic Science Service. All the FSS labs were the same. All the FSS labs had formal peer-review. They all have quality standards, and peer-review is an absolutely essential part of any forensic science report after you've done the work".

CHAPTER 21

Safeguards

Peer-review

Peer-review is a long-established method of ensuring quality. "Well I think we always did it", said Professor Barclay. "Since the first time I joined in the early 70s we did peer-review, but it was formalised certainly prior to the Lynette White case and the person who was responsible for that I think was Dr Brian Rees. He was the person who was in charge of quality assurance in the FSS and he was our Deputy Director at Birmingham. He came from Chepstow spookily enough, so I find it very difficult to believe that they didn't have the same systems in use in Chepstow, because Brian Rees came to our lab from Chepstow".[1] It is strange that this safeguard was not extended to forensic pathologists for several years. Barclay played an important part in achieving that.

"Peer-review involves getting your assistant to agree that you've interpreted the results correctly and you write it up and then you get somebody who's normally your immediate superior to check the content, which is that everything in that is correct—you haven't made any slips, but also that what you've said in the report is actually what you meant to say", he said. It can therefore weed out unexpected problems, which at first glance may not seem important, but in actual fact are of great significance. Professor Barclay gives a poignant example, explaining how

1. Barclay is referring to a strange anomaly that occurred in the Lynette White Inquiry. The work of forensic scientist Dr John Whiteside had apparently not been peer-reviewed in that case—the usual evidence of peer-review, counter-signing the report/statements was absent from Whiteside's statements made under the Criminal Justice Act. This was sufficiently odd to grab Barclay's attention. It suggested that peer-review had not happened in this case. It has not been explained why that happened, especially in such a controversial case. At the time of writing it is unclear if the statements were peer-reviewed but not recorded properly, or not peer-reviewed at all.

The Lynette White Inquiry resulted in a grotesque miscarriage of justice. For further information on it refer to my books **Fitted In: The Cardiff 3 and the Lynette White Inquiry** and **The Cardiff Five: Innocent Beyond Any Doubt** (2nd Edn., 2017), both of which are still available—the former from **The Fitted-In Project** (http://fittedin.org/fittedin/?page_id=15) and the latter from **Waterside Press** (see https://www.watersidepress.co.uk/acatalog/Cardiff-Five-Sekar-2nd-Ed-9781909976528.html).

it established that a scientist was not communicating effectively. That in turn affects the questions asked and evidence given, which obviously could affect the verdict too.

"Now that's a very tricky and big distinction, so it's not just that the words make sense and they're justifiable with the physical results, but do they actually convey to somebody reading it what you meant to convey?" he said. "And I was very hot on that when I was head of a department at Birmingham. I had one member of staff who was almost incapable of writing what she meant to write and that was a very bright person with a PhD who ended up actually not doing casework. She wasn't making any mistakes maliciously. She wasn't making any mistakes writing up her reports, but the impression her reports gave was not what she thought she was saying, or what she meant to say. Her English wasn't good enough to accurately convey what was in her head and that's very dangerous of course, because if she was cross-examined about that she would be able to justify it, but that still might leave a misleading impression to the jury, so my recollection is that she was given a new role outside casework".

Sanctions

Nobody would suggest that such a scientist should be sanctioned. As Professor Barclay says, "She hadn't made a mistake. She hadn't fiddled things". She hadn't, but what about more sinister examples? What should happen to them and what role should the Regulator have in ensuring accountability? "To get back to the Regulator, I think anybody who actually does make a mistake and tries to conceal it, or who deliberately writes a report which is meant to be deceptive should be permanently stopped from doing casework", Barclay said.

Just that? "Well it depends, I guess after that", he said. "That's the internal side of it. After that you come into legal sanctions—well, is it perjury? Is it conspiracy to pervert the course of justice, or whatever? So after that point you come into ordinary legal battles. If you thought somebody had deliberately lied in court that is perjury".

The peer-review system was around since the early 80s, at least. Some of the notorious miscarriages of justice from that era and even earlier were in the era of peer-review, but it failed to stop the application of dubious techniques and even work—for example the now infamous Griess Test.

"Let's deal with the Griess Test in the Birmingham Pub bombings case (Birmingham Six)", Professor Barclay said. "It's almost a technical matter. It had almost unforeseen consequences, but it should have been picked up, yes. It should have been picked up in my view by the technician, possibly in Chorley because that's where the tests were done. In those days the assistant wouldn't have been as involved as they were in Birmingham, *but it should have been picked up if an assistant was used, and if not, by the peer-reviewer*. It was a technical slip which had far reaching consequences. The Griess Test business was something that should have been picked up. You're absolutely right" [his emphasis].

PART FOUR

CONSEQUENCES

"The time for action is now. It's never too late to do something".

Antoine de Saint-Exupéry

CHAPTER 22

Exceptions

Perverse Logic

The Forensic Science Regulator cannot look at individual cases. That raises the question of whether the FSR has sufficient powers. Professor Barclay mentioned the case of Dr Alan Clift in the previous chapter. His initial fall from grace came over an individual case. That resulted in an internal review, which identified several other failings, which in turn resulted in Clift being sanctioned. This may be a missed opportunity, as there does not appear to be any body that investigates potential abuses in individual cases, or even clear ones relating to these cases. Such regulation could at least prevent repetition. It has been suggested that there were flaws in the peer-review process in the Lynette White Inquiry. I have been informed that Dr John Whiteside's statements in early 1989 had not been counter-signed, which is the pre-requisite of peer-reviewing. It is unusual, to put it mildly, and triggered investigations in the Phase III investigation to try to establish exactly what had happened and what the explanation for the apparent lapse was. It is not clear whether it had, in fact, been peer-reviewed and the paperwork was just shoddy or whether there was a more sinister explanation. It also raised the issue of whether anything similar had happened in any other case that Whiteside had been involved in. I have been reliably informed that enquiries were pursued to check that, and some of Whiteside's other cases written before and after were looked at. I have seen no evidence indicating that any of those cases were not peer-reviewed.

So what does this mean? It suggests that the Lynette White case was an exception. It was either peer-reviewed and the paperwork was not up to the required standard — a cock up that only the peer-reviewer can explain — or there is a more sinister explanation. Whiteside's crucial statements were not peer-reviewed, despite the requirement to do so. If that occurred, it is a very significant matter — one that requires explanation.

Peer-review exists for a reason—to catch and correct mistakes. It should happen and any time it does not, it must be explained. If peer-review was avoided deliberately in this case that would be very significant and very worrying, but peer-review is at most part of the story—the icing on the cake—even though it would be astonishing that it happened in such a notorious miscarriage of justice.

The Curious Thing

"The curious thing about John Whiteside's case was that for eight or nine months he was working on the basis that it was a single male that had stabbed Lynette White, that that male had cut himself during the act and had spread blood at the scene", Barclay explained. "Remember there's no DNA, or DNA's just coming in. He identified the blood on the wall as cast-off, exactly the same as Angela Gallup did and exactly the same as I did. That's why that bloodstain was targeted in particular. He also identified that since the body had been dragged, blood on the socks and the bottom of the trousers might well be the offender—a mixture of course of offender's blood and Lynette White's blood. Suddenly, he changed his mind about that, *and he changed his mind about that, because he discovered that the blood groups from Angela Psaila, who was a person associated with Lynette White, were exactly the same as the blood groups that he got from the wall at the scene* and those blood groups were 1:3800 or 1:7600 depending on whether you take into account that it's male blood, so let's say it's one in 3800, he jumped to the conclusion that that blood had come from Angela Psaila" [my emphasis].

But it required absolutely perverse logic to believe that Psaila's blood groups *proved* she was there at the time. The cocktail-hypothesis, as it came to be known, was important scientifically, but its significance for both Barclay and Whiteside was not just in a scientific context, but more so in the context of the case itself. It was a possible explanation of the blood grouping evidence, but opinions on its credibility differed greatly. Was it a credible explanation in the context of other possible explanations for the foreign blood? The Phase I investigators relied on the cocktail-hypothesis. It was the only explanation offered for the presence of that foreign blood at the crime-scene, but it applied to only one area of one bloodstain. There was at least one other — the sock — that was known to be foreign and consistent with the blood grouping results reported on Area 4 of the bloodstain (JAW14) on the jeans. There were other bloodstains that were foreign too. Was the cocktail-hypothesis likely or probable in this context? Was Psaila's combination of blood groups really that significant in the context of the case if all of this information was taken into account?

"Well, it's crucially significant only if you look at it from the wrong way round", Barclay said. "If you think Angela Psaila is one of three or four friends of this girl. Her blood is at the scene — blood matching her at the scene — well that cannot be coincidence *he is thinking*. Of course it *could* be coincidence because the blood groups could have come from thousands of people in the area, not just from the friends; and it actually *was* coincidence. Not only that, but it didn't actually match her because we now know that it contained male material and DNA that was completely different, but from a blood grouping point of view, he regarded it as being such a coincidence that it must be significant to the case" [his emphasis].

Failure

However, the scenario that Whiteside convinced himself was the explanation of the results was actually ludicrously improbable. The original and correct case-hypothesis — one man acting on his own — was never disproved. In fact, it was eventually proved to be true when Jeffrey Gafoor was unmasked as the real killer — the evidence from the crime-scene was only consistent with one man acting on his own, regardless of explanations that appeared to try make inconvenient facts tell a different story. That emphasised the extent of the travesty of justice that had occurred and also the failure of the safeguards that ought to have prevented it from occurring. Professor Barclay conducted reviews of the scientific evidence. He explains what went wrong.

"The police then manage to produce for him evidence that Angela Psaila had been bleeding from the mouth and at that point John Whiteside had another difficulty because there is no saliva test obtained from that blood on the jeans, or any of the other foreign bloodstains though maybe it's gone off, or there isn't any", Barclay said. "It's not in a sensible position — there's no spitting on the floor of blood and saliva, which you would expect if somebody is bleeding from the mouth. The pattern is completely wrong. There are no drops on the floor on the way out. Drops are on the wall where it would be cast-off from the hand and, crucial point, Lynette White has bled out on the floor. There are no footwear marks in blood from, as it turned out, eight or nine people who must have been charging about in a darkened room where she must have bled all over the floor. Really, *that is ludicrously improbable.* John Whiteside would never have thought of that scenario in the first place. I mean people would have laughed at him had he said right from the start without the evidence of Angela Psaila's blood — 'I think it's eight or nine people have done this and they've been charging around here stabbing her and stuff like that.' Nonsense" [my emphasis].

Whiteside's hypothesis was improbable at best even in 1988, but it got worse later. DNA testing conducted during the Lynette White Inquiry Phase II proved that there was far more foreign blood in that crime-scene than was known about in 1989. Could all of those bloodstains have been explained as a mixture of Psaila's blood with that of an alleged male killer, and if so how had that happened? Even without the proof that it was Jeffrey Gafoor's blood, the methods used to locate these bloodstains were not rocket science and they were not dependent on DNA testing. They were validated scientific techniques that had been used for many, many years. It has never been explained why the conclusions drawn from blood distribution patterns by Professor Barclay and by Angela Gallop of Forensic Access from evidence available in 1988 were not drawn then by Whiteside and others in 1989.

Whiteside's cocktail-hypothesis was scientifically ludicrous now and also in 1989, so how was this not picked up in peer-review? After all, the process was designed to pick up mistakes. "I did a review of this case for South Wales Police", said Barclay. "I couldn't find any evidence in the paperwork that was supplied to me, which included a manuscript draft of his statements, that that particular case had been peer-reviewed. It's sufficiently unusual to grab my attention. So I asked South Wales Police to look at 100 cases before and a hundred after the Lynette White one and to my recollection they found that every one of them had been peer-reviewed. *The only one that the usual evidence indicating that it had been peer-reviewed was absent from appeared to be this case, which, as far as I know, is the only one which there is serious doubts about the sense of the report's conclusions*" [my emphasis].[1]

1. At the time of writing I am awaiting confirmation of whether Whiteside's 1989 Criminal Justice Act statement(s) had been peer-reviewed or not and if not what conclusions can be fairly drawn from that. If it is proven that peer-review did not take place, as appears to be the case, was that a cock up caused by sloppy paperwork, or is there a more sinister explanation? On any view, the paperwork should be up to the required standard and the safeguard should perform as intended, or it cannot work as desired.

CHAPTER 23

Coincidence?

Serious Failing

Could the apparent failure to peer-review Dr Whiteside's work in the Lynette White Inquiry have been a coincidence? We may never know. "They just, on my instructions, found out whether cases were peer-reviewed and I was informed that they were in every case apart from the one I was investigating, Lynette White", Professor Barclay said.

It is unclear exactly what had happened. The usual evidence of peer-review — the countersigning of the witness statement by the peer-reviewer, and if an assistant was involved in the work, that person too, was conspicuous by its absence in the paperwork that was provided to Professor Barclay, which included the witness statements made by Whiteside in early 1989. Whatever has happened, this was an extraordinary failure that ought to have been picked up far earlier, whether the report/statement was peer-reviewed or not. Both Whiteside and the person who was supposed to have peer-reviewed it must have known both the established procedure and whether peer-review had occurred or not. The paperwork should reflect this. If it was peer-reviewed, then it should have been counter-signed, no ifs nor buts. And if it was not peer-reviewed then the person who should have peer-reviewed it must also have known that it did not occur. If that occurred, why didn't that person raise the alarm, both with Whiteside and higher up if necessary? Why did it take several years for the apparent failing to emerge?

So how did it happen? "My recollection is John Whiteside was interviewed under caution for two days and he, I believe, and again this is just from my recollection, said he couldn't remember why", Barclay said.

Astonishing. This is the only known example of a case of his where the usual evidence of peer-review is absent. At the very least the safeguard had not performed as required. This was a high profile case with a very controversial case-hypothesis, so who would have been responsible for peer-reviewing his statements? "It should have been his immediate superior — the boss of the biology department at Chepstow, or the Assistant Director, because it was quite a famous case, so maybe the Assistant Director would have been the person", Barclay said.

This makes the apparent failing even stranger. If Barclay is correct, it should have been known about at a high level within the Chepstow Laboratory. That person must know if he or she peer-reviewed Whiteside's statement or not. It should be made clear if that happened or not, even at this late stage and the failure to countersign should be explained, even now. If it turns out that Whiteside's statement was not peer-reviewed, then the failures which occurred must be explained and consequences addressed as best they can be after such a long delay.

Consequences

If ever a scientist's work required peer-review, this was it, because Whiteside had changed his opinion drastically and there did not appear to be a credible reason for doing so — the evidence had not changed — it still has not. The evidence remained consistent with his original opinion — one that was never proved false — and subsequently that opinion, rather than his controversial one, was proved correct. An extraordinary change of opinion, especially in a case like this, should have had a very good reason to justify it. Quite simply, it did not. Psaila's combination of blood groups was actually an irrelevance, rather than 'one hell of a coincidence', as Whiteside claimed. There was no evidence whatsoever that proved Psaila's blood had been shed in the flat during the murder and there was evidence that could have tested the controversial hypothesis, such as blood distribution patterns and amylase activity — the test for saliva — that suggested that the cocktail-hypothesis did not stand up to scrutiny. These methods of testing the cocktail-hypothesis were never applied and these were precisely the type of points that should have emerged during peer-review. If peer-review occurred, it failed to perform as it should have, and if it did not happen, that is a very serious failing. So what are the consequences for failing to peer-review?

"My strong recollection at Birmingham is that you could not get your reports typed if they weren't peer-reviewed, so they would be returned to you if they weren't signed off", Barclay said. "That was part of the process, so again that's a bit strange because again I believe that all the labs were doing more or less the same thing at that time and that's perhaps indicated by the fact that all the other cases were peer-reviewed".

So why didn't this ring alarm bells?

"I have no idea", Barclay said. "I wasn't there. I mean all I can say is that it seems that it wasn't and it should have been and the point of peer-review is to pick up exactly this sort of thing. You have to draw your own conclusions about why that one case does not seem to have been peer-reviewed".

Sinister?

If it had been known by the defence lawyers at the trial of the Cardiff Five that there were serious queries over peer-review, it surely would have been investigated then and raised at trial, so who bears responsibility for this failure—the scientist, his boss, both? Should the institution itself take responsibility?

"I actually don't think it does, because if it set up a system that should work, what you're talking about is not corporate responsibility for it, you're talking about somebody making a mistake", Barclay said. "I guess legally they are responsible for their servants, aren't they, so they have some responsibility, but I don't think they have responsibility in a culpable sense if they've set up systems which somebody has decided to circumvent".

But that depends on establishing whether it was circumvented and if so, whether it was deliberately avoided and who else could have prevented that from happening—that is where organisational responsibility becomes an issue. So how should a 'lapse' like this be dealt with? "I really don't know, but the ultimate peer-review is in court, because you have to stand there and defend your report in front of people that are asking you questions that you don't know what the questions are going to be in advance, so that's pretty strict peer-review if the defence knew what it was doing", Barclay said.

The situation at the relevant time needs to be clarified too. The ultimate peer-review opportunity was in 1989 and 1990 when the Cardiff Five were tried for the murder of Lynette White. Defence experts were instructed, but it is not clear exactly what was disclosed to them. If they did not have the actual statement that would have been counter-signed, they would not have known that there was a possible issue. They may have seen the lab-notes and other material, but that is not the issue. The results and actual evidence are not and were not in dispute — it is the interpretation of those results that has been questioned. The defence experts could have questioned the cocktail-hypothesis. They did that. They found it possible, but unlikely. They could have gone further and perhaps should have done. The methods used by Barclay to question it were available to them too. However, they could only have known of possible failure to peer-review if they had access to Whiteside's original statement that required counter-signature — a typed copy would not suffice.

Barclay is clear on the responsibilities of a forensic scientist. "That's why I think that the little chink there — the thing you have to bear in mind — it's not enough to rely on the defence asking the right question of you", he said. "The forensic scientist has to raise all these things themselves, which is why I think Dr Clift was wrong not to give the other side of the story about the blood grouping in the Preece case, and it's why I and other people at Birmingham certainly would have volunteered any weak bits in our case before we were asked by the defence, because the defence are not always capable of asking the right questions".

Lack of Consequences

But that did not happen. Whiteside's hypothesis was exactly the type that needed peer-reviewing. Whether that happened or not, despite that being standard procedure, it is clear that any peer-review could not have been robust enough. There were and remain very clear concerns over Whiteside's cocktail-hypothesis that should have been thrashed out in peer-review. It remains unclear if that ever happened. It affected the cross-examination too, as Yusef Abdullahi's defence had no idea that the usual evidence of peer-review was absent from his statements and because of that they never asked the question of Whiteside or the Assistant Director of the Chepstow Laboratory or even his immediate superior there about it. Despite many official inquiries or reviews the apparent failure to peer-review has yet to be explained.

Whether it was sinister or not, it illustrates two things. First, the importance of peer-review itself and second, that without consequences for not peer-reviewing, it could happen again. Also, it is unacceptable that the apparent failure to peer-review was not raised until around fifteen years later, and only then because of further investigations caused by the vindication of the Cardiff Five. And remember that forensic pathologists were not even subject to peer-review themselves when Jeffrey Gafoor was convicted of the murder of Lynette White.

CHAPTER 24

Errors and Procedures

Weeding Out

Peer-reviewing is an important safeguard. If working as intended, it can help to identify and rectify errors, but to achieve that there also has to be consequences if it has not occurred. The correct procedures must be followed and if that has not happened, then the reasons for any failure to follow them must be established rapidly. If the cause of the failure was cock up rather than conspiracy, then the resolution should reflect that, but if the motivation is deemed to be sinister, there should be severe consequences. There are lessons to be learned from the Lynette White Inquiry over this.

Some sort of lapse over peer-review appears to have occurred and there seem to have been no consequences at the time it mattered most — during the trials of the Cardiff Five. Barclay raised the apparent lapse years later and it was investigated by the Phase III team. There is no doubt that peer-review was an established procedure within the FSS at the time and that Whiteside knew this. It plainly should have happened and the paperwork should have reflected that it had occurred, if indeed it had. The system, introduced by Brian Rees, was so strict in the Birmingham Laboratory that reports would not even be typed if it hadn't been done. He had been at the Chepstow Laboratory previously — the one where Whiteside worked. So what happened? At the time of writing it is unclear whether it was in fact peer-reviewed as required and for some reason the report was not counter-signed as it should have been, or whether it was not peer-reviewed at all. It clearly should have been. The situation is further complicated by the decision of the Coalition government, headed by David Cameron, to shut down the FSS — that has resulted in any answers as to what happened being archived.[1] It is to be hoped that this will be investigated thoroughly.

Safety Nets

If it did slip through the net of peer-review, it is astonishing that it happened in such a high profile case and that it was not discovered for more than a decade — it was first raised during Professor Barclay's review of Whiteside's work for South Wales Police. This was far too late for the ultimate peer-review of the trial of the Cardiff Five. The apparent failure to peer-review was strange — if they were not peer-reviewed, they certainly should have been — and it requires explanation, but the main issues remain the controversial explanations advanced by Whiteside in December 1988, and in his subsequent witness statements in 1989 and at both trials of the Cardiff Five.

Peer-review, which is now mandatory for forensic pathologists, can only work as intended if the consequences for failing to observe it reflect the gravity of the failure. If peer-review was avoided for sinister reasons, then that must result in severe repercussions, including criminal sanctions if that is deemed appropriate, but that will depend on the credibility of the report to be reviewed. Errors can be easily and honestly made. Peer-review can detect those and correct them painlessly, but where the conclusions reached are not sustainable by the science and other evidence, avoidance of peer-review may well be deliberate and therefore evidence of something more sinister. If that is the case, it must be weeded out rapidly and fearlessly.

"There can be errors in forensic science and albeit we are working now with a much more robust quality standards framework, which has started to deliver and demand much more accountability", said the former

1. Since the collapse of the Lynette White Inquiry Police Corruption Trial in 2011, there have been three inquiries into the case. None of them have focused on why the original miscarriage of justice was allowed to occur. There has also been the attempt by police officers involved in Phase I to secure compensation. That case ended in failure in June 2016. The interpretation and manipulation of the forensic pathology and crime-scene evidence is detailed in **Appendix One — Interpretation or Manipulation**. Reviews were conducted on Whiteside's work by the FSS and also by Professor Barclay — the latter for South Wales Police. Neither of those reports have seen the light of day. They should be published without delay: **The Editor**.

Forensic Science Regulator Andrew Rennison.[2] "It does not inoculate us against science failings, but it does put around it a whole quality framework that massively mitigates against the risks of that happening".

But does it? It did not appear to have worked in the Lynette White Inquiry, although that happened over a quarter of a century ago.

Advances

Forensic sciences have advanced considerably since then, but what about quality controls? The Lynette White Inquiry shows the need for robust quality controls, but how is that to be achieved?

"What you've also got to remember is that case law in this country and the advice of senior judges is: 'Yes we do want to see science that is valid and fit for purpose, but also we want to leave the door open for new science in the courtroom, because it is still very common'", Rennison said. "The rate at which science is advancing in this day and age, it would be wrong to restrict the courts in their use of new and emerging technologies and judges allow that, but they are developing quite a robust way of handling that within the courtroom, so it's not the processes that I want, it's through case-law that judges have recently established a very robust process for judges to establish the quality of that science and to manage it accordingly".

The courts helped to set the terms that scientists must operate under through case-law — a procedure Rennison approves of. "That's proper use of the procedure rules and a very, very clear framework developed in the case of *Reed and Reed* [2009], by Lord Justice Thomas"[3], he said, "and he's reminded people recently through other published judgements that he's made that this is how the courts should manage expert's evidence with particular reference to forensic science evidence. So yes, errors can happen, but we now have a quality standards framework at the front end. We now have the criminal procedure rules, which are designed to properly manage experts through the prosecution and trials process and

2. **The Fitted-In Project** interviewed Mr Rennison in 2010 and again subsequently.
3. Currently, Baron Thomas of Cwmgiedd, Lord Justice (Sir John) Thomas became President of the Queen's Bench Division in 2011, and, Lord Chief Justice (LCJ) on October 1st 2013. He was succeeded as LCJ by Baron Ian Burnett of Maldon on October 2nd 2017.

clear reminders from the Lord Chief Justice[4] and Court of Appeal through recent case decisions that that process has got to be properly employed. We've now got recent case decisions through the Court of Appeal that demand a far more robust examination of the admissibility of science records and its split into the quality of the evidence—the quality of the science and the competence of the individual to give that evidence and the case of *R v Whelan*, I think it is, talks about the competence of the individual".

Such measures should help, but the problem in Whiteside's case was that the failure of the peer-review process—either through inadequate paperwork, or an actual failure to follow the correct procedure of peer-review slipped through unnoticed. It was therefore impossible to raise this at trial. Could this happen again despite the improved procedures?

4. Baron Igor Judge was the Lord Chief Justice at that time.

CHAPTER 25

Quality Standards

Case-law

Case-law provides additional safeguards to peer-review and trial processes. Rennison could not eliminate the possibility that errors will occur, but was confident that the updated procedures are working.

"So to summarise; it could happen, but there are far more checks and balances right the way through from the front end all the way through the inquiry through to prosecution and court process because the courts are heartily fed up with poor quality expert evidence", Rennison said. "There is also the review of the Law Commission on the admissibility of expert evidence, published in April [2010]. They are now at the stage where they are about to publish their final report and draft legislation to give the courts more powers to admit or deny expert evidence in the courtroom to the criminal courts, so it's a very different paradigm nowadays, thankfully. I'm happy that it can be prevented through everything that I've described, through standards framework for the front end, through proper use of the criminal procedure rules at the middle level and through increased powers to the courts through the legislation, and case-law to manage the admissibility of expert evidence".

Rennison is also concerned with the science. "We also have me able to now investigate the quality of the science", he said. "There are other examples where the Court of Appeal have sought my advice on the quality of science, not in individual cases, but with science issues they're trying to resolve, so it's another plank that is now thankfully being employed and we have a Crown Prosecution Service who are much more alert to their responsibilities to the use of science. I regularly meet the CPS Policy Lead on forensic science issues and she agrees with me that they've got to increase their level of interrogation of the science that they employ in prosecutions, because they're equally fed up with cases like this historically that let the prosecution down".

But it is in individual cases where this science is applied and where mistakes in delivery will occur as they did both in the science and quality management in the Lynette White Inquiry. It has to be remembered that the failure in the interpretation of the science, expertise, and in the quality management over the forensic science in that case, has never been addressed and it appears that there is no intention of ever doing that. But individual cases are the concrete test in practice of whether these systems work.

Prevention

The Regulator has a role in preventing miscarriages of justice, so how would this be done? "By putting in place a whole new quality standards framework and the focus actually — since 1995 — the laboratories have themselves adopted a good quality standards framework", Rennison said. "One of the gaps in it since '95 has been the police in-house functions and police laboratories, so the Code of Practice I published is focussed very much on getting all laboratories, including police laboratories up to the same standard and I now have regular meetings with the police and are working with them to roll these standards out across their laboratories — in house laboratories, where they're not so much doing analytical work; they're doing evidence sampling work. We now also have a decision — European decision — what they call a framework decision, which will have to translate into UK domestic law within the next few years that demands accreditation to the standards I'm stipulating".

So what would the Regulator have done differently in a case like this where there are clear concerns over the forensic science, peer-reviewing of the expert's work and quality management? "Very difficult question to answer", Rennison said. "With the benefit of hindsight, clearly the investigation should have been handled differently — the whole investigation. I think with the benefit of hindsight, better use of alternative expertise. I think we should be prepared to consult with other people to see what other experts have to say and look at the validity of the advice you're getting. I think it's what I would have done differently at that time".

CHAPTER 26

Reassurances

Public Confidence

Clearly, miscarriages of justice, especially notorious ones, affect public confidence. Forensic sciences have advanced at a rapid rate. Things thought to be science-fiction just a decade or so ago are now routinely conducted and there is no reason to believe that DNA, for example, has reached the limits of its potential. So why should the public believe that previous errors that bedevilled inquiries in various scientific disciplines, including pathology, have been consigned to history?

"Well, we are using vastly superior technology nowadays — the new DNA technology — and there is a robust quality standards framework around it, which gives more accountability at the organisational level and we are developing that by the day, so my job is to put a robust quality standards framework around all of it — around all forensic science — so we don't just look at DNA, but all forensic science", Rennison said while he was the Regulator. "We're now looking at fingerprints. We're looking at shoe-mark evidence. We're looking at tyre evidence. We're looking at every form of forensic science evidence and the quality that should be wrapped around it. That does not remove all risks, I'm afraid to admit, but it manages the vast majority of them in a very robust fashion".

But how does the Regulator ensure that the lessons of individual cases, especially ones that used old-fashioned techniques, but which were subsequently resolved correctly, or even capable of resolution, are learned?

"We do look back at cases as examples, but I tend not to go back as far as '88, '95 and 2003, because the world has moved on considerably since then, so we tend to look at more recent cases, from which we should learn lessons from", Rennison said. "Damilola Taylor and Rachel Nickell and other cases, and Sean Hodgson — it is an historic case where issues have come to light recently, because looking back too far in history means you are actually reviewing science that is very out of date anyway, so your reviews has got to keep up with the technology".

However, forensic science played a crucial role in resolving 'historic' miscarriages of justice and cold cases. That raised issues affecting other cases, or at least could have done, if their methods were applied. Nothing illustrates this better than the limbo cases—ones where convictions have been quashed, or acquittals secured, but the cold case reviews have something to lose. Resolution by the conviction of real offenders in these cases illustrate the failures in original investigations. Better, some say, to let sleeping dogs lie. Forensic science cannot and should not tolerate this. How can lessons be learned if nobody looks for them?

Equality of Arms

An example of the problems associated with the short-sighted approach is the monopoly over the National DNA Database. The Lynette White Inquiry is not the only very serious crime to be solved by innovative use of that Database. Police had the DNA of the perpetrator—there was no doubt about it, but what happens if there is no match on the Database? You can shrug your shoulders and hope that it will be resolved in the future, or do as South Wales Police did and take a pro-active approach. Familial DNA proved to be the key. While neither Joseph Kappen, nor Jeffrey Gafoor had their DNA profile stored on the DNA Database, close male relatives had—Kappen's son and Gafoor's nephew. This told police the family that the killer belonged to in both cases with one important difference. Kappen was already a suspect, while Gafoor was not. The discovery of the significance of his nephew's DNA profile told police that the killer was one of his close male relatives. Why can't these investigative methods be utilised in other cases such as the limbo ones? Why shouldn't defence lawyers have the right to have the DNA Database checked? And there are other significant matters too.

"Well I think that lies equally with the Criminal Cases Review Commission and their ability, because once you get the cases finished with appeals process, there's no more lawyers can do", Rennison said. "It then hands over to the Criminal Cases Review Commission and what I'm really happy with is their ability now to come to us and experts I can refer them to, to look at the science. You know, Forensic Access, who I think helped with the paint issue you described,[1] I put the CCRC in touch with people like that and other experts we know and trust out there, who can advise on some historic cases, but there proved to be a very, very powerful facility and ability for me to sit down with the CCRC Commissioners and discuss these old cases. It equally applies to the unsolved cases — the Cold Case Reviews — and I do know that some police forces will equally go to a company like Forensic Access and say nowadays: 'Will you help us with a cold case review of this'? You tend to find that the very best forensic scientists have the breadth of mind to look at new ideas and new things and we do encourage that. It's very important. You will remain reliant on the professionals you employ".

However, the limbo cases are a different matter. They depend on the will of police to actively investigate a case where they know that resolution will open their force to scrutiny of the original investigation. History has shown there is not the will to look into these cases. The Lynette White Inquiry remains the only one in England and Wales that was correctly resolved without a cold case hit pointing police in the right direction first.

1. Blood had been preserved under paint for fourteen years in the Lynette White Inquiry. DNA was obtained from it. It could not have been planted. It was Jeffrey Gafoor's DNA. Confronted with the overwhelming DNA evidence Gafoor pleaded guilty. The fact that certain types of paint preserve blood and DNA was important.

CHAPTER 27

Smoke Without Fire

Limbo

Some parts of the criminal justice system don't want to go back and look at the limbo cases, because they know that correctly resolving these cases will prove that there is no doubt that it was a miscarriage of justice. That explains the reticence and why there needs to be an independent body to look into these cases, especially in an era where even quashing a conviction is no longer seen as meaning that the appellant has been exonerated.[1]

"Well I think that's a valid point because these cases are handled differently", Rennison said. "Where you do actually find the true perpetrator as happened in the Lynette White case, you are able to close a case. You are able to say actually these people are conclusively innocent. Often you're left with that question mark hanging over you, aren't you? That decision's by people other than me and I'm pleased to say that forensic science nowadays can do more and more to help that. Actually the technology is helping more and more in these cases".

But is it? It can only help if there is the will to investigate. There's no shortage of limbo cases. Perhaps an independent body is necessary to investigate these cases.

"That's a difficult decision", Rennison said. "That's the sort of stuff you've got to take to the Home Office. I'd like to think if ever that body

1. It is in everybody's interests to resolve these cases and learn lessons from them to prevent repetition, as nobody is protected in homicides that have not been solved and this category includes some notorious crimes. It is also in the fiscal interest, as the sooner lessons are learned and, where necessary, changes are made to the criminal justice system that help to deliver justice to all concerned and prevent the waste of resources of pointless inquiries designed to gaze at the entrails of limited aspects of cases rather than in these cases in the round. For example, despite resolution in seven homicide cases in the UK in the DNA age not one of them has had a thorough review of the whole case after resolution. How could the lessons be learned without such review in proven miscarriages of justice cases? And then there are the potential lessons—totally ignored at present—in the limbo cases with the added problem of refusing to release reports on the basis of a claim that to do so would prejudice the prospect of resolving these cases. These decisions are made by police with no independent scrutiny of the justification.

was set up, modern forensic science would prove very helpful to them. Forensic science is available to anybody who wants to use it and the advantage of modern forensic science is that actually it is totally independent of all of that. It is science that helps you. True forensic science helps you to get to the truth of these matters in a way that it couldn't in the past and that's my role in this. I'm quite happy that people choose to use this for all sides, but I'm hoping to promote the use of modern forensic science. That is one route to doing that".

But forensic science alone cannot make the difference; it requires the will to turn stones many would prefer remain unturned. The failure to research familial DNA is a classic example of this.

Familial Investigations

The investigative commitment shown by South Wales Police to resolve the Llandarcy rapes and murders from the 1970s and the Lynette White Inquiry was exemplary — a model for any investigation that does not get an immediate hit after a check on the National DNA Database, not just the limbo cases. Professor Dave Barclay explains not only the potential, but what has been achieved to date.

"It's not likely that they're the only two, because we have used familial DNA in other live cases and therefore by definition there would be familial DNA in other 'dead' cases", Barclay said. "The first time that it was used [in a live (current) case] was the brick through the windscreen that killed the lorry driver on the M3, and the brick was done for DNA.[2] It wasn't from the actual person, but it was a relative that was on the database, but then when the sample was taken from the kid, it matched completely, so the familial DNA is just a way — an intelligence way — of getting a short list of people who might be relatives of the real person. You still need to get the actual DNA from the person. Now in most cases if this crime had been committed by somebody with criminal convictions, they might be on the database anyway in the UK, so you're

2. Michael Little was killed after a brick was dropped by Craig Harman through the windscreen of his lorry, while driving on the M3 in March 2003. The impact of the brick on his chest caused enough damage to Little's heart to kill him. Harman was traced through familial DNA — a hit to a relative that identified his family and led to Harman who was convicted of manslaughter in April 2004.

likely to get a direct match, so you're only talking about DNA samples left at the crime-scene from somebody who is a relative of the offender, but the offender is not on the database and that won't be that many".

That is certainly true, but the point remains that in cases that do not produce a direct hit on the National DNA Database, that need not and should not be the end of the story. There is no reason why the method used to help to tie Joseph Kappen, Jeffrey Gafoor and Craig Harman to their crimes cannot be used in any case where DNA has been deposited at a crime-scene by the perpetrator, but that person is not on the Database. In each of these cases it involved a small quantity of DNA, sometimes degraded DNA. This illustrates the importance of all the procedures involved in preserving both evidence and the integrity of such evidence. Forensic pathology is certainly an integral part of that process.

CHAPTER 28

Challenges

Optimal Efficiency

There is no question that advances in forensic sciences have been made at a rapid rate. That shows no sign of slowing. It poses new challenges, not least of which is ensuring that the organisation and provision of forensic science remains optimal in the UK. "We have in the UK quite a unique model for the provision of forensic science", Rennison said. "The traditional model around the world is for science to be delivered by a central government owned laboratory or laboratories and that's what happens all around Europe apart from the UK. We now have choice, but within that model, it is usually the police who manage the forensic science at the front end, so they manage the crime-scene. The police usually have control of all fingerprint technology. Beyond that they bring in the government laboratories. In the UK we now have that model — sorry England and Wales — but we don't have the government laboratories now. That brings with it strengths and weaknesses". Another obvious problem is the monopoly on choosing providers of forensic science services. To whom are police accountable for the choices that they make and how is that accountability delivered?

Rennison, however, welcomes the diversity of forensic science providers now. "One of the major strengths of this is a competitive market, so it is driven by efficiency and driven down cost, so now we're seeing effectively more routine use of forensic science, because it's better and it's faster and it's cheaper, so you've brought commercial acumen into a traditional government supplied market", Rennison said. "The weaknesses that comes with it is that it's decreasing the amount of money being invested in forensic science and also for research and development for the future, because in the past the routine forensic science had money around that was helping to prop up research and development, so we're looking at ways to question that at the moment. Scotland has a totally different model, where all the crime-scene investigations and all the laboratory investigations are managed by one organisation, which is the Scottish Police Service Authority. Northern Ireland has a slightly different model. They're all different. They all have strengths and weaknesses".

Making a Difference

But what does Rennison want to see done differently? "If I was to design a perfect model for the UK, I would want to enhance the commercial market, particularly with the products—pile them high, sell them cheap—which we do now with DNA technology, because of the whole automated lines, so we've got good quality around it", he said. "There's no real difference between good quality technology and what we now do in building good quality cars. It's modern automated lines with robotic controls, with all the quality controls in place, which are driving efficiency up and costs down. It doesn't work in complex cases, but I'd like to see a commercial market. The optimal model would be a commercial market where it's needed, but with some government laboratories to manage the complex cases. Some of that is under review at the moment. I don't think we'll ever end up with that, but I think that would be the optimal model, so you can drive the advantages of all different systems into one system and drive out some of the weaknesses. We do lead the world in modern forensic science and we are now beginning to lead the world on the quality framework". However, global considerations have to be considered in the delivery of an optimal organisation and provision of forensic sciences in the UK, despite the different systems.

A common framework, or at least one that allows comparisons to be made across borders, must be applied in the delivery of forensic sciences, as co-operation across borders requires standardisation of procedures and provision of the sciences. It is especially important in these confusing times regarding the relationship between Britain and the rest of the European Community. At least some of the welcome procedures adopted in Britain are due to that relationship and the need to standardise procedures and systems regarding the science in the era of easy movement across Europe. Freedom of travel within Europe has resulted in convicted criminals traveling freely to other European countries where they have a clean slate. Britain has been on the receiving end of such crimes, but equally, British criminals have emigrated to new hunting grounds where they have committed crimes. Various countries use different DNA testing systems. They involve common loci (genes that are tested), but this affects the discrimination power (random match statistics). The European DNA Profiling group (EDNAP) has been instrumental in achieving a degree of standardisation of loci tested regarding DNA. Obviously it applies to other forensic sciences as well.

PART FIVE

REVIEWS

"The more you explain it, the more I don't understand it".

Mark Twain

CHAPTER 29

Organisational Accountability

Responsibilities

So far, accountability has been on an individual basis. Forensic scientists, including forensic pathologists, must be held individually responsible for the quality of their work. Peer-review is part of that process. Sadly, it was not mandatory for pathologists until around 2004. But what about organisational responsibility? The top forensic pathologists were allowed to describe themselves as Home Office pathologists. That conferred status upon them, but what about the Home Office? What responsibilities should that impose on the Home Office to ensure that the quality of work conducted by these pathologists is up to standard? What is required to deliver organisational responsibility?

Rennison suggests a solution. "Accreditation for all DNA laboratories and all fingerprint enhancement laboratories", he explains. "Now our DNA labs are meeting the standard, but the fingerprint labs aren't. We now are agreeing plans for the police to get there, because they're all police run and it's down to the police to get all those labs up to the standard, so what we're seeing is a move away from the ad hoc approach we had historically and it was managed by a lot of different people through different methods, none of which linked together to a single coherent quality standards framework, which is bringing all the labs up to the same standard, but it has one key component, which was never in the ad hoc framework in the past, which is accountability at the organisational level, because forensic science is very rarely produced by individuals working alone in their garden shed".

Rennison is determined to impose standards that extend beyond simply holding individuals responsible. "Scientists give the evidence in court, but the way they undertake their work, the way they are recruited, the way they are trained, developed, the way they're managed and the way their work is audited is all done by the people that employs them", Rennison said. "It is a well-accepted fact nowadays that the quality of the science evidence coming out of the organisation is as much influenced by the culture of that organisation as it is influenced by the competence of the individual scientist and that is broadly accepted fact, so the framework that I'm implementing is demanding far more evidence of its organisational competence".

The Consequences of Disorganisation

The consequences of organisational failings are clear. An individual case example where the safeguards failed is the Cardiff Five—a case cited by Rennison. "Well in the Cardiff Five case, the forensic science I think skewed the thinking", he said. "I must choose my words here. You say 'skewed the thinking' in your books, and I agree with that, and that was because an individual in a powerful position within a forensic science organisation was allowed to really do their own thing and I don't see much evidence of organisational control around what that individual was doing. And that had a huge impact on the rest of the inquiry and then they got drawn into supporting the inquiry, so objectivity didn't seem to exist, did it? I think had they been able to stand back and had their work been properly peer-reviewed at the time, and I don't think that work was ever properly peer-reviewed, it would have had a different outcome".

This was the point. The safeguards should have prevented a scientifically unsustainable explanation from being allowed to skew the thinking and with it the case too. Whiteside put forward a scientifically ludicrous hypothesis as fact. It was a case-hypothesis that should have been halted in its tracks long before it reached court—before it set in motion the wheels of injustice at break-neck speed. Whiteside's hypothesis should have been torn to shreds in peer review. If Whiteside's hypothesis was an error, or just over-enthusiasm at a discovery that he thought was more significant than the evidence suggested, it did not add up in scientific and evidential terms. It should have been detected and halted in peer-review. That cannot have happened as it was advanced in evidence. Whether peer-review occurred or not, it cannot be said to have functioned as intended. The cocktail-hypothesis should never have passed peer-review. Either it was not peer-reviewed as it clearly should have been, or somehow the flaws in Whiteside's hypothesis were not picked up in peer-review. It had dire consequences too. The case against the Cardiff Five was flawed, to put it mildly. One of the biggest problems was the 'foreign' blood. It had plainly been shed during the murder, so how could it be explained?

Blood grouping tests established that it had not been shed by any of the men who stood trial in 1989 and 1990. DNA testing confirmed that too, which was proven later by the further more sophisticated DNA testing. There was no question that that blood had not been shed by any of the Cardiff Five on their own. A creative explanation was required to explain the seemingly inexplicable. Professor Barclay has shown that the police's case-hypothesis defied logic. It was improbable to the point of impossibility, because the crime-scene evidence and blood distribution patterns could not be reconciled with so many alleged killers and participating witnesses in the circumstances that the crime was committed. Other problems with Whiteside's interpretation were raised by other FSS scientists too. This involved meetings at the FSS Chepstow Laboratory. Among those to raise concerns were DNA experts Nicholas Prance, and Prance's boss, the Head of Biology at the Birmingham Laboratory Trevor Howitt. Concerns were raised about the statistics for the blood grouping results. The cocktail-hypothesis was certainly considered in meetings with Dr Peter Gill, whose 'sex-determination' test was very sensitive for the presence of the Y-chromosome. One area of the foreign bloodstain on Lynette's jeans was tested using Gill's test. The Y-chromosome was detected. The evidence was clear, but that left interpretation. Various possible explanations were considered and eliminated with reference to Psaila such as blood-transfusion or chimera.[1] They also considered the possibility that it was male blood — never conclusively eliminated — and that it was a mixture of male and female blood. The sensitivity of Dr Gill's test was such that any positive result could be explained as a mixture. The possibility could not be excluded by Gill's results, but what about when considered as a whole? There was other foreign blood in that flat.

1. Chimera is named after the beast in Greek Mythology that was part lion, part goat and part serpent. In terms of DNA it means a single being that has genetically distinct cells. It can be visible in animals. Examples of chimera include people with both male and female organs, or two distinct blood types. It is rare in humans. See http://citeseerx.ist.psu.edu/viewdoc/download?doi=10.1.1.149.9001&rep=rep1&type=pdf for further information.

Was that a mixture too and was there sufficient opportunity for Psaila's blood to have mixed in intimately with that of a cut killer before being cast-off? If this could occur, what quantity of Psaila's blood would be required to obscure the differing blood grouping results of the alleged male killer in such mixtures? Was any amylase activity detected on any of these foreign bloodstains? It remains unclear if anyone ever raised these issues with Whiteside and if so, how he answered them. It is also unclear whether the FSS took organisational responsibility to ensure that his report and evidence accurately reflected what the evidence was consistent with.

Consequently, this was far more than an individual failing. If it was not peer-reviewed then not only Whiteside, but the scientists who should have peer-reviewed his work, especially in a case of this magnitude, must have known that peer-review had not taken place, so why wasn't it raised with Whiteside, or higher if necessary far earlier than Barclay's review? And if it was peer-reviewed, why had it not been counter-signed? Why did the normal practices break down in this case of all cases?

The FSS later conducted a review of Whiteside's work in this case. Alistair McPhee, then working at the FSS Laboratory in Chorley, reviewed Whiteside's work. The FSS refused to disclose this report, which was critical of Whiteside. It is unclear if it explained what had happened. The FSS failed to ensure that Whiteside's report and the evidence that he gave at trial was scientifically credible and provided the most likely interpretation of the evidence. As such it must be held responsible and as it was accountable to the State, ultimate responsibility must be borne by the State itself.

CHAPTER 30

Absurd

Nonsense

It was obvious, or should have been, that Whiteside's hypothesis could not be sustained by the science or the crime-scene evidence. What should have been a clear scientific picture had become distorted but how had this been allowed to occur?

His hypothesis was palpably absurd, but as Professor Barclay explains, it did not matter a whit. Barclay demonstrated in practice that Whiteside's original hypothesis was consistent with the evidence, and that there never was a plausible evidence-based reason to abandon that opinion, especially in favour of an outlandish hypothesis that had no basis in forensic science. There were several reasons to believe the single-male killer hypothesis, based on an integrated approach to the evidence, and no credible reason to abandon it, especially in favour of a hypothesis that was, according to Barclay, "scientifically ludicrous".

Barclay now thinks that the lack of challenge to Whiteside's change of opinion from a perfectly routine single male explanation, to the eventual extremely improbable hypothesis including Psaila and many others, is the key to what went wrong.

Critical Appraisal

"Irrespective of any peer-review or lack of it, how did John Whiteside justify this change to other scientists in Chepstow and Birmingham?" Barclay asks. "Did no-one critically examine the change, and way he worded his statements based on his new hypothesis? We know that both the reviews, mine and [Alistair] McPhee's, were seriously concerned about this very point".

These are exactly the type of things that peer-review was designed to stop in its tracks, but whether Whiteside's statements were peer-reviewed or not, the deeply flawed hypothesis was put forward by Whiteside in evidence as a credible explanation of the foreign blood. That should never have been allowed to happen. His employer bears some responsibility too. They should have established exactly what went wrong and corrected it—after all, rightly or wrongly, it tainted the reputation of the FSS as well. This was a miserable failing by Whiteside and also the FSS.

CHAPTER 31

Reviews

Inadequate Review

The Lynette White Inquiry is a sorry tale. It was the first miscarriage of justice — conventional definition — in a homicide case to be resolved in the DNA age in Britain. Aspects of it have been reviewed by different parts of the criminal justice system. None have had public input, let alone scrutiny. This includes the forensic science. As we have seen previously, there is an urgent need, as the manipulation of the scientific results was essential. The miscarriage of justice required the turning of four people into crucial witnesses. That began with Psaila. Eventually, she had to be deceived into believing that she had been in the room when Lynette was murdered and that had to be achieved, despite her certain knowledge that she had not been there when it happened. It was so thorough that she insisted during the trial of the Cardiff Five that she had witnessed the murder and taken part (non-fatal cuts) because her blood had been found in the flat. It had not been, but police had convinced her into accepting a lie as fact because of Whiteside's hypothesis. At some point the FSS conducted a review, by Alistair McPhee, then of the Chorley Laboratory. He had concerns about Whiteside's work too. The Chorley Lab was closed by the Coalition government as part of the abolition of the FSS. The closure has caused difficulties in locating McPhee's report — it is unclear if any of the post Police Corruption Trial reviews considered it.

Despite two reviews of very limited aspects of the Lynette White Inquiry and a third into the same thing, the scientific failures that were crucial to securing the miscarriage of justice have not been reviewed. South Wales Police certainly investigated Whiteside's role during the Phase II and Phase III investigations, but during the latter the CPS chose not to prosecute. As with much else it has never explained this decision and the government has never explained why a full review of the whole case is unnecessary, especially as all the reviews that have touched on the forensic science are either inadequately explained or still remain behind closed doors.

The Chorley Review

"The Forensic Science Service (FSS) conducted a thorough internal review at the time of the original appeal", said Lisa Palmer, then a spokesperson for the Forensic Science Service. "In line with normal practice the review was conducted by a scientist from a FSS laboratory not connected to the original work. In this instance, it was conducted by a scientist working at the FSS's laboratory in Chorley". The scientist was McPhee. "The FSS was satisfied that the work had been conducted in an appropriate manner and that the science was sound according to techniques commonly used at this time".

It is impossible to believe this. The science was anything but sound as demonstrated by Professor Barclay's masterful demolition of Whiteside's hypothesis. Sadly, the FSS was far from finished with their damage-limitation exercise.

"No specific recommendations were made as a result of the review however it is the case that the technology with respect to body fluid identification and comparison had advanced greatly with respect to sensitivity and specificity between the time of the offence and this review", Palmer wrote.

This is worrying and irrelevant. If no recommendations were made in a case where the work of its scientist fell far below the required standard, and had equipped an unscrupulous investigation with the information required to indulge in conduct a leading judge described as 'unacceptable in a civilised society', then something is seriously wrong with the body that failed to make recommendations. Whiteside's nonsensical hypothesis enabled the police to convince Psaila that an outrageous lie was truth, although police claim that they did not tell Psaila about her blood in the crucial interview after they had been told about her blood groups. Really? Why did she incriminate herself then? It is far more likely that this was the straw that broke her resistance and with it that of the other alleged eye-witnesses. Whiteside's work was unethical at best. It was also essential to the execution of the conspiracy.

Evasive

The FSS continued to try to evade responsibility and also the questions asked of them. "The work in this case was managed in line with the normal working practices that were in place at the time", Palmer replied.

Firstly, that was not true and secondly it very obviously didn't answer the questions asked, which were: 'Were Dr Whiteside's findings peer-reviewed as was normal practice within the FSS at that time?' and more importantly, 'Does the FSS support the interpretation that Dr. Whiteside put on his results in 1989, even though the scientific evidence did not support the five killers hypothesis, or even the cocktail-hypothesis (this was verified during the re-opened investigation of 1999–2003.)?'

If Palmer's responses accurately reflect its views, then the FSS failed miserably in its responsibilities.

McPhee's report has never been released to the public, despite the collapse of the Police Corruption Trial and review processes, and even the abolition of the FSS. The conclusions cited by Palmer are not what I have been told it says. There is no reason to withhold it, especially in these circumstances. Lisa Palmer's response on behalf of the FSS does not resolve the issues raised, especially in the context of McPhee's report. If her interpretation of it was true, it means that while Barclay saw several flaws with Whiteside's interpretation of the evidence — others too — McPhee did not, so who was right? The evidence suggests that Whiteside's interpretation was wrong at best and was in fact unsustainable on the evidence — an integrated approach to the forensic sciences and crime-scene evidence would have shown that. Consequently, if the FSS was satisfied at the time and subsequently with Whiteside's work, even though it was scientifically ludicrous, that indicates serious organisational failings within the FSS.

CHAPTER 32

The Blame Game

Pervasive Culture

Safeguards are essential to prevent miscarriages of justice and also to ensure that public confidence remains intact. Juries, and the public as a whole, must trust the system if justice is to be dispensed. It is a crucial issue. Maintaining erroneous convictions helps nobody, but trust must be earned and then maintained. Scandals like the Lynette White Inquiry do nothing to achieve those goals. The forensic science was actually clear. It tried to tell the story of Lynette's murder and actually did. At first Whiteside listened to it, but then a coincidence occurred and Whiteside allowed that to dominate his thought processes. It over-ruled scientific logic completely. Instead of the weight of evidence and scientific logic bringing Whiteside back to reality as more test results emerged, he stuck rigidly to his hypothesis, justifying the scientifically ludicrous—failing time after time to realise that it simply did not add up. Why was this tolerated?

"There is something that suggests that wasn't peer-reviewed, because I know there was some work done around peer-reviewing before and after and this one appears not to have been, but it asks a really important question about the organisation that recruited him, trained him, employed him and supervised him, but allowed him free reign to operate the way he did", the former Forensic Science Regulator Andrew Rennison said. "I think the same thing happened with Dr Frank Skuse in the bombing incidents—the terrorist incidents—where there was a lack of organisational control. That all pre-dated the quality controls that the Forensic Science Service put in place in the early 90s".

Organisational Culpability

Whiteside's conduct offers a warning, but one that Rennison believes offers a big lesson. "If you go back to cases like this one and it happens in your book,[1] the questioning goes to the individual scientist", Rennison says. "The same happened in the Birmingham bombers, the Guildford bombers and other miscarriages where science was to blame. The focus was back on the individual scientist. I argue and I'm supported by friends in America on this, Professor William Thompson, who's a professor on psychology in California — he's written a brilliant paper on this — he and I both argue that actually, you shouldn't adopt what he calls the bad apple syndrome, focussing on individual bad apples. You should look at it through the lens of organisational theory and organisational psychology". Rennison has a point. There is plenty of blame to go around. "It focusses on this historic blame culture in the past that blamed individual scientists and never ever looked at the organisation that was supposed to be managing them", Rennison says. "A much more robust approach, I argue, is to hold the organisations accountable, so we should be holding Chief Constables and the Directors of laboratories accountable for the quality of the forensic science they deliver and that's the framework that is in place. That's one way of managing miscarriages of justice, but we've got to recognise how forensic science works in the criminal justice system and a focus on the past is on the wrong parts of it. We are now focussing it very, very differently with a view to driving out these miscarriages".

Vigilance

Further vigilance, as Rennison points out, is required. "What we've got in place now is an ability to manage the hearing now, both with the framework to look to the future to make sure that forensic science is very robustly managed and we've also now got a window back into the past where there is a suggestion of previous miscarriage to advise and I've deliberately now placed three of my scientists working within the Criminal Cases Review Commission", he said. "Their staff, their investigators in the past, had to go to outside experts to ask about the science.

1. **Fitted In: The Cardiff 3 and the Lynette White Inquiry** was published by **The Fitted-In Project** in 1998. It can be ordered through the **FIP** at http://fittedin.org/fittedin/?page_id=15 and **The Cardiff Five: Innocent Beyond Any Doubt** (2nd Edn., 2017) is available from the publisher **Waterside Press**. See https://www.watersidepress.co.uk/acatalog/Cardiff-Five-Sekar-2nd-Ed-9781909976528.html for further details. **Trials and Tribulations: Innocence Matters?** can also be ordered from **The Fitted-In Project** as above.

They come to us now. We give them freely available advice on science matters, which they find enormously helpful. I'm in the lucky position of having a very good working relationship with the police. I have a very good working relationship with the Crown Prosecution Service. I have a very good working relationship with the Criminal Cases Review Commission, with the Law Commission, with the Fiscal Commission, so I've worked very hard to develop stake-holder relationships right across the whole breadth of forensic science and prosecutions and reviews of historic cases—all in terms of the quality of the time".

As Rennison points out, the Lynette White Inquiry, or at least Whiteside's role in it, is an old case, based on old scientific techniques. It is unlikely to be repeated, but it highlights flaws in the safeguards. There should have been no doubt about whether Whiteside had been peer-reviewed or not, and if for any reason it had not occurred, he should not have been able to avoid or evade that safeguard. There were more flaws in his approach and that of the FSS than just the apparent errors over peer-review. It is not simply an individual failure on his part. The FSS failed to redress these wrongs, even giving responses which appear to have been economic with the truth. That is unacceptable. The ultimate peer-review of trial depends on adequate disclosure, which did not occur in this case. Both forensic scientists instructed by the defence in the original trials, and also appeal, did not have access to all of the material that they needed. That is also unacceptable.

CHAPTER 33

The Challenges of Advances in Technology

The Promise of the Future

The Lynette White Inquiry shows that forensic science has advanced in leaps and bounds. DNA testing was rudimentary when she died, but fifteen years later it was crucial to solving it and other cases too, but not in isolation — the relevant DNA had to be located and that involved methods that were available in 1988.

"DNA technology as it has emerged over the last two decades with all its strengths and all its weaknesses — it has been heavily contested in the courts — has been very effective at overturning miscarriages of justice, so people who were innocent have been proved innocent by the use of DNA", Rennison says. "Forensic science in this case was able to solve it through use of more modern DNA technology and effective use of that as well and you've got to recognise it's all well and good having the technology; you've got to have scientists who can use it effectively, because what we are doing now is that new DNA technology enables you to analyse microscopic amounts of DNA, so much so that you will never know what sort of cellular material is the source of the DNA. You won't know whether it was sperm, whether it was skin, whether it's from saliva — whatever it is. You can trace that DNA back to an individual, so that's the area we are talking about — a handful of cells here".

This is extremely important. An infamous miscarriage in the Netherlands, the Schiedammer Park crimes, illustrates the need for procedures and careful adherence to safeguards. In June 2000, ten year-old Nienke Kleiss was raped, stabbed and also strangled with a boot-lace — the lace had been taken from the boot of her eleven-year-old friend Maikel Willebrand (she had gone to the park with Willebrand to play with him. Willebrand had also been viciously attacked by the perpetrator Wik Haalmeijer. Willebrand survived by playing dead. The fact that there were two victims and a perpetrator made this a complicated investigation. The forensic science would play a vital role in resolving it. Haalmeijer strangled both victims. Less force was used on Willebrand, as the boy used his wits to survive by playing dead. Kleiss fought back and was subjected to greater force which in turn aided the discovery of DNA.

The strangling aspect of the vicious crime was crucial. This is the investigation that Dutch DNA expert Richard Eikelenboom referred to previously. It was clear from the pathology evidence that strangling her involved the use of considerable force. That in turn meant that contact DNA of the perpetrator would be likely to have been transferred onto the lace and that would prove to be vital evidence. Eikelenboom was aware of this and developed the protocols to extract the DNA and obtain DNA profiles from it and other areas. There was no question that they succeeded in obtaining the killer's DNA and that it eventually made resolution of an egregious miscarriage of justice possible, yet it also raised new problems as the very strengths of these new advances in forensic sciences were also the dangers.

Obvious Problems

The problems were obvious. There were two victims and a perpetrator at the scene. The crimes were committed in such a manner that the cells deposited by the killer were contact cells—epithelial cells (skin)—and those had to be located and extracted first. These are notoriously difficult to locate and extract and required the protocols described by Eikelenboom. "No scientist ever likes DNA mixture from three persons, but in this case it was inevitable that we had to look for that and the other problems with blood and bronchial fluids from the victim was very likely and then skin cells coming from the hand of the perpetrator and you know there is 85% chance of getting profile from blood or fluid and only 16% chance of getting it from epithelial cells", Eikelenboom said.

Clearly the difficulties were immense, but not insurmountable. "16–20%", Eikelenboom said, "so very small chance of it containing the profile and then 90% of your material contains DNA of your victim. And in terms of your perpetrator, even if your perpetrator is in there, you won't be able to see it. You won't get it, because if there is too much DNA, if it is amplified too much, you won't get much perpetrator DNA.

That's very important. We had a project with LCN. I had a lot of power around there on this, more or less, so I introduced LCN DNA for the first time. I helped to solve this case, so the preliminary work on LCN DNA was done here. All the profiles here were obtained through LCN DNA. On the boot-lace, which as I found on the neck of the victim — the cord — we look at DNA markers (alleles) and we look if these numbers did not match the two victims, then okay, maybe it is coming from the perpetrator. So, we found strange alleles not matching the two victims on the boot-lace. We found them on the fingernails as well. What's more important on the nails is she was a nail-biter, and we found nothing else and I know because I sampled them. So, that means we know that all DNA was on top of the fingernails and that also means if they were playing in water as Maikel [Willebrand] describes, then it is very likely that DNA on top of the fingernails was shortly before she was killed (i.e. after they had finished playing)".

These methods show that important results can be obtained from very small amounts left from contact by the perpetrator on skin and clothing and, crucially, from ligatures, such as boot-laces. It therefore offers an opportunity to solve homicides — ligature strangulation — involving laces, or even clothing. This opened a new world of opportunity, but it requires not only the new procedures, but integration of forensic sciences. This is exactly what happened in the UK case of the 'Worlds End' murders from 1977, of which Angus Sinclair was convicted in 2014. The very sensitivity of these methods, however, means that contamination, whether accidental or deliberate, is a real risk.

CHAPTER 34

Brave New World

The Challenge

The challenges posed by the advances in forensic sciences have to be understood and met. The sensitivity of DNA testing is one of its great strengths, but also a potential weakness—one that offers a defence of contamination.

"Well of course it is because you then have increased opportunity for contamination, for mixed profiles", Rennison said. "You've got to have a clear understanding about the transferability of DNA, so the fact you've been here will leave your DNA here. Does that mean that if somebody else sits in that chair and then goes and sits in another chair that they'll take your DNA with them? Well that's got to be understood. We shook hands earlier. Have we transferred DNA? Well some people transfer more than others. Some people shed; some people don't, so all of that's got to be better understood and you've got to manage those risks, so the standards that we're putting in place where they [the police] recognise that right from the crime-scene, we've got to have very, very tight procedures to manage your collection of DNA samples all the way through the process because you cannot afford the excuse of contamination".

As Rennison implies, contamination is a potential defence, or rather explanation, of DNA being found at a crime-scene. The question is whether it is plausible or not? "I've even gone through the system to the crime-scene", Rennison says. "In the more recent past the problems we've seen in the DNA world is actually contamination introduced by the swabs. The cotton swabs that you use to recover DNA already have DNA on them. They might be medically sterile swabs, but medical sterilisation doesn't eliminate DNA, so you've got that additional process in play to make sure that they are DNA free".

Chastening Examples

There is a chastening example on this. Even though Professor Barclay is not so concerned about contamination, because the significance of DNA traces must always be assessed in context anyway, he acknowledges the infamous exception that wasted masses of police time and led to a bogus hunt for a serial killer that never existed. It occurred in Germany. They thought they had found some evidence of a prolific serial killer, but it turned out to be contamination. "Yes in the actual swabs that were used", Barclay said, "but they didn't identify a serial killer. They didn't think anybody had actually done it. They just wasted a lot of time and I think that's the issue. There's a lot of loose talk about contamination".

'Contamination' is normal and need not be sinister. "I watched a video of a Northern Ireland bomb investigation involving an examination of one of the timer powers units (TPU) and we knew that the technician involved had got his DNA on some of the items inside the power unit", Barclay said. "So we had some transfer of DNA from one of the people who examined them into the inside of one of the timer power units. We couldn't understand how this happened. We watched the videos. The whole thing was videoed. The people were gowned up and gloved up and about the third time we looked through the videos we saw the person who was handling it stretch his back, scratch behind his ear and carry on working on the bomb and people had watched that at the time and they'd watched it on the video and they hadn't seen it. Because if you scratch behind your ear with your gloved hand, you've now got your DNA on the outside of your finger that you used to scratch your ear and now you've gone and touched material inside the bomb and you've transferred your DNA to the inside of the timer power unit. *It's not sinister.* So that's why we all, including myself, even though I've long retired, every time I go and examine something at a forensic lab I have to give my DNA, because it's impossible to prevent what's called 'contamination' — it's actually just transfer" [his emphasis].

It's why everyone who handles exhibits has their DNA recorded, but as techniques get more sensitive the possibilities of s*econdary* transfer greatly increase and that is a real problem. But assessing the significance of any forensic results means you have to take account of other possible explanations anyway. This is what John Whiteside really failed to do in the Lynette White Inquiry regarding his cocktail-hypothesis.

New Dawn

Rennison is not swayed—he believes that contamination is an important issue, or rather the procedures to prevent it, or at least reduce the risk, are important.

"We are leading the way", he says. "There's a whole new process in place on swabs and reagents that you bring into the crime-scene, so we eliminate that—we think we've largely eliminated that, but we've got to be absolutely sure, so that was all part of the question of what are your opinions of the way forensic science helped to solve this case. It was new technology, but we recognise now that there's a whole new range of risks, so in '88 and '95 there was a range of risks".

The challenges now are great and require efficient procedures as the problems of the past are replaced by new issues. Rennison is acutely aware of this. "They've largely gone now, but this new paradigm brings a whole new range of risks, which is about guaranteeing the integrity of this trace evidence all the way through the system and we're working very hard on that", Rennison said. "The forensic science labs have very good processes in place and the police are very good as well and I'm tightening up on all of that because the courts—and these cases help with this—fully accept the validity of DNA technology. They accept it is a very robust science that's very effective in the criminal justice system. I'm absolutely determined that there shouldn't be earthquakes happening because of poor handling of DNA that can dent that confidence. We had it and we had to do an independent report with scientists to evaluate the use of DNA, so the confidence was dented then. It's back up now".

He was talking about the Omagh Bomb case. Although the trial judge had made a number of adverse comments, the science was in fact vindicated by different reviews. However, poor procedures were allowed to happen in the Lynette White Inquiry and chance after chance to establish what happened was wasted. John Whiteside's statements should have been counter-signed, confirming that they had been peer-reviewed—the usual practice. They were not. It has never been established if they were peer-reviewed or not, even though there were several opportunities to check. The issue was raised during the Lynette White Inquiry Phase III investigation. Before then there was a CPS review of the case against the Cardiff Five, an old-style committal hearing, two trials of the Cardiff Five, the appeal of the Cardiff Three, an internal police review, the reopened Lynette White inquiry (1995–98), and also the Lynette White Inquiry Phase II (1999–2003) which ended in the conviction of the real murderer Jeffrey Gafoor. Phase III of the Lynette White Inquiry included the trial of the alleged eyewitnesses Mark Gromek, Angela Psaila and Learnne Vilday, as well as the so-called Police Corruption Trial. After that there were investigations by the IPCC and HMCPSI. The QC Richard Horwell's Report into why the Police Corruption Trial collapsed was delivered in July 2017 — it had been delayed until after the police officers' civil action against South Wales Police was completed. Not one of these processes dealt with the scientifically ludicrous hypothesis and the consequences of the poor procedures that allowed it to skew the thinking.

CHAPTER 35

Risks

Contamination

Professor Barclay offers a different perspective on the dangers of contamination to that of Rennison. "People talk about contamination", Barclay explains. "Routinely samples get 'contaminated' in a laboratory, which is why all the laboratory staff have to give their sample. If I contaminate a sample over the years with my DNA because I've handled it in the lab, what that does is reduce the evidence against the suspect, because it means you have to subtract my alleles from the alleles that arose actually during the crime, so contamination is actually an issue which helps the defence, helps the actually guilty, not leads to mistaken convictions (unless the real offender works in the lab, of course!)"

Barclay believes, and he is supported by scientific review on it, that the science associated with Low Template DNA is sound. But he goes further in terms of the dangers of contamination. "It's a bit of sophistry used by defence to explain things sometimes, but in fact, in general, all it does is reduce the value of the physical evidence and if you've got the right person that means it's reducing the value of the prosecution case, and it's a normal thing", Barclay says. "We mustn't think of it as contamination. I mean I could have a face mask and be handling items in the laboratory and I suddenly cough sufficiently to move the face mask off my nose, that's a situation which you can get 'contamination'".

He worked on a number of cold case reviews, including Omagh, the Lynette White Inquiry and another infamous one.

"Angus Sinclair got off due to a logically ludicrous decision of the judge in the World's End Murders—all three I'd been really involved in and all three sort of went down almost at the same time", Barclay said. "It was pretty well disastrous. I'd spent years of my life doing those three cases. The Omagh Bomb, the judge's rulings were eventually over-ruled by other people who investigated the science and the context. Angus

Sinclair has now been convicted of the World's End Murders because they did double jeopardy on it".

Aspects of the forensic science in the Lynette White Inquiry are being considered again to determine what action, if any, needs to be taken in relation to it.

Omagh

It was by any description a very controversial inquiry. Sean Hoey stood trial and was acquitted on the orders of the judge Mr Justice (Reginald) Weir. Forensic scientists and police officers who had been wrongly criticised remain incredulous at the verdict and criticism, which was rejected by the Ombudswoman for police in Northern Ireland. Barclay is among those perplexed by the decision.

"The judge made I think four determinations in the Omagh bombing trial which led to the defendant being released", Barclay says. "I mustn't say he was found innocent; he was found not guilty. Of course in Northern Ireland, it's a single judge. I think all four of his decisions on the *physical evidence have* been subject to review and have *all* been found to be *not correct*. Even—I think it's—Nuala O'Loan, the [Police] Ombudswoman in Northern Ireland, did a review to the alleged contamination issue. He admitted that he'd made bombs previously and the defence suggested that his DNA found in timer power units might have arisen because the lab had possibly contaminated things and there was some suggestion that some documentation had been altered to conceal something" [his emphasis].

So, were the alterations to the documentation deliberate and sinister or not?

"She [O'Loan] came to the conclusion that the documentation was just a slip", Barclay says. "It wasn't completely relevant to the argument about whether it had been designed to conceal what might have been contamination; and the contamination issue couldn't have happened anyway. It couldn't. It's just nonsense. It was very difficult to understand the judge's decisions and there was a big investigation I think, maybe involving Brian Caddy—a sort of independent forensic investigation and that came to the same conclusion that in fact the difficulties with the case were illusory and existed only in the mind of the judge".

So what has all this got to do with forensic pathology? It illustrates the need for their work, skills and expertise to be integrated into modern investigations, and be subject to effective safeguards. The days of Spilsburyism and Spilsburyesque investigations belong to history.

PART SIX

SOLUTIONS

"If there is no struggle, there is no progress".

Frederick Douglass[1]

1. Douglass was born a slave. He escaped aged 20 and played a formidable role in the fight against slavery in the USA from the 1840s and Jim Crow discrimination in the 1890s. He was the author of three acclaimed autobiographies—*Narrative of the Life of Frederick Douglass, an American Slave* (1845), *My Bondage and My Freedom* (1855) and *The Life and Times of Frederick Douglass* (1881). Douglass was also the editor of a successful black newspaper for sixteen years, and an inspiring orator too. He was a firm believer in equal rights, both racial and gender. He was appointed Consul General to Haiti and Chargé d'affaires to Santo Domingo (now the Dominican Republic) in 1889 by President Benjamin Harrison. He resigned in 1891.

CHAPTER 36

Primacy

Procedural Problems

The previous insistence on primacy of forensic pathologists led to Spilsburyism, but for all his flaws, and there were several, Spilsbury was certainly a very able pathologist, technically. The same cannot be said of others, yet they still exploited Spilsbury's demand for primacy. Professor Barclay gives a good example of the dangers of the primacy mentality affected by slack procedures.

"I can think of one, with a pathologist who I believe was later removed from the list, where a body was found and on the scene video you can see his feet walking round the body and then the body is turned over and he's walking next to where the body had been", Barclay says. "This is before anybody else had a chance to take footwear marks, fibres or anything".

Such scant respect for established procedures, and indeed the importance of evidence, is and was even then — decades after Spilsbury died — completely unacceptable. However, Barclay points out that such practices have now been eradicated. "Now that attitude has gone", Barclay says. "I'm pretty confident that's gone completely and in particular I can give you a good example of why it's necessary for that to have changed. Supposing you're stabbed and I'm looking for fibres and hairs to link you to the offender — the contact points, because it's a close contact crime — if I allow the pathologist to have primacy and he wants to turn the body over to take anal swabs or something like that or he wants the body removed because it's in a dangerous place and he wants the body taken away in a body bag, well, that loses that fibre and hair evidence because when I said you've been stabbed, you're leaking. You leak all over the inside of the body bag and that removes the fibres from where they were originally and loses all the contact point evidence, so it's got to be the SIO who decides, 'no in this case, we won't let the pathologist touch it until it gets back to the mortuary—we will tape it for fibres at the scene'".

Some pathologists fought change tooth and nail, but it was an idea whose time had not only come, but was essential for the reasons that Barclay mentions. "I think that's a big change and it's quite a sensible change too which was always good practice by most pathologists anyway, and has been reinforced by the need to prevent DNA transfer", Barclay says. "In the UK as a matter of routine, we would tape the body at the scene and it would be a forensic scientist that would do that. Then you get in the situation where you can remove the body without losing further evidence".

This explains why the primacy mentality that had pervaded the thinking of forensic pathologists for decades—the best part of a century—had to go, but self-regulation? When has that worked? Peer-review is designed to stop egregious error and if functioning well, it will do so, but it is a form of self-regulation and self-regulation has a long and wretched record of failure. Peer-review itself failed in the Lynette White Inquiry. Something had plainly gone wrong. There is no evidence that Whiteside's work was peer-reviewed. He may even have deliberately evaded it. His statement was not counter-signed by the peer-reviewer as was required. Nobody has accounted for this discrepancy, which took years to emerge. The FSS never took responsibility for it—even to find out why it had not been counter-signed. The FSS staff who should have peer-reviewed Whiteside's work must have known that it had to be done. If they did not receive it to peer-review, they did not raise the alarm. There is no evidence that the FSS or police informed the defence through the CPS that there was a discrepancy, let alone establish if it had been peer-reviewed as was required. It remains unclear if it had been peer-reviewed or not. It is difficult if not impossible to be certain whether it was peer-reviewed or not. Consequently, the safeguard was ineffective in this case and one can only wonder how many other times this has happened, and if it will be as effective as intended in the future. It only emerged because the role of Dr Whiteside was reviewed again in a different process—one that most cases do not get. There were no consequences for whatever happened regarding peer-review in that case. So what other options are available?

Roles

Professor Barclay would like to see the Forensic Science Regulator have a greater role.[1]

"I think he has a role about governance as it is, but I think it should almost be like—I was going to say the Financial Services Authority, but they're not a good example to use", Barclay said. "He should have teeth. I don't think forensic scientists deliberately make mistakes, or fiddle evidence, but I would say that wouldn't I? I have been a forensic scientist for 35 years, but when they do, or if there are failings in their processes which lead mistakes to go through the system, then I think something serious needs to be done about it to rectify the systems. It's not just a question of a mistake being made, but there are systems in place to prevent them getting through. And I would like the Forensic Science Regulator to have those powers to suspend people from doing casework or to stop them doing casework completely and there have been instances in the past where the Forensic Science Service, as it then was part of the Home Office, voluntarily did that".

Of course, Whiteside's conduct regarding peer-review may not have been a mistake. Whether it was or not, the consequences were dire. It shows why independent regulation is essential.

1. This has now happened. As a result of reviews referred to previously, the Forensic Science Regulator is on the Home Office Pathology Delivery Board, which took over from the Home Office Policy Advisory Board in 2005. Its Constitution was approved in 2012 and amended in 2015. The function of this Board is clearly relevant, as are the various reviews, Hutton (2015) Wassermann (1989) and Leishmann (2003). All of these will be reviewed in the forthcoming **FIP** publications **Forensic Pathology: Righting Wrongs** and **Forensic Pathology: Next Time The Fire**.

CHAPTER 37

Time for Change

Pathology Comes of Age

Professor Sir Bernard Spilsbury was long dead, but Spilsburyism took longer to be consigned to the grave. Forensic pathologists saw themselves as above and aloof from the investigative process. That had to change. Professor Dave Barclay, saw the problems with this approach sooner than many others. He recognised the need to integrate forensic pathology into the investigative process, kicking and screaming if need be. For most, it was welcome and reinforced what they were doing anyway, for others it required being dragged into the requirements of modern investigative techniques.

"When I was Head of Physical Evidence at National Crime Faculty from '97 onwards, part of my job was to do reviews of previous cases—cold cases and so on—and also live cases, and I became uneasy that some pathologists weren't getting as much as they could have done out of the cases and that seemed to be actually worse the further north you went in the country and it was obvious that the reason for that wasn't any incompetence by the pathologist", Barclay explained. "It was that they didn't regard themselves as an integral part of the investigation, so they were thinking more about what the cause of death was—putting it very simply—rather than what the pathologists and the SIOs in some areas wanted to know, which was rather that they, the SIO [Senior Investigating Officer], wanted to know everything that led up to the cause of death".

Forensic pathologists had tended to limit themselves to their traditional areas of expertise and expected other experts to be almost subordinated to them. That was a legacy of Spilsbury and Spilsburyism. It would never be tolerated in the DNA age. Public confidence alone would see to that, along with the CSI-effect that had grown in that era. Juries demanded DNA in virtually every case. That was not the pathologists' domain and it wasn't what SIOs wanted either. They — at least the good ones — knew that DNA could not be supplied on demand. If it was located, extracted and explained, well and good, but that would not happen in every case. Other forensic sciences may be required. It was horses for courses and the days of the pathologist holding court as Spilsbury had done were over. Not only that, but SIOs expected more from pathologists too.

"The cause of death is vital for court, but it's almost a formal thing", Barclay said. "What you want to know is has the girl been chased? Has she bounced off a wall? Has somebody hit her first and then she's run away and then she's been smothered somewhere else? So, what the SIO is interested in — Senior Investigating Officer — is pretty well everything that led up to the cause of death and not quite so much the technical cause of death and that means a mind-set which sees the pathologist as part of the investigation".

Investigative Pathology

It was clear that a change was due. "In my experience at Crime Faculty, that approach varied a lot across forensic pathologists", Barclay said. "As a result of the unease about that, I had a Memorandum of Understanding with a group of pathologists which included Nat Cary and his practice, which was I think at the Fulham Pathology Services, or something like that. They were somewhere in Fulham and in fact keen to take part in case conferences at an early stage of an investigation. So, they were routinely asked to peer-review the work of other pathologists, often in historic cases and we also did the same thing with somebody called Iain West, who was at that time probably the most famous pathologist in the UK until he died in the early 2000s I think. He worked with his wife Vesna Djurović. Now Iain possibly was a little too definite sometimes. He was a bit Spilsburyesque in stature in some respects in the view of courts, but he was doing that because he was trying to think what the SIO would want to know, so he was interested in marks on people's faces, had he been hit, had he been stamped and so on?[1] He would be

1. West was involved in a case where he clearly got the cause of death hopelessly wrong, and failed to answer very important pathology-related questions. Even now, 30 years on, these questions remain unanswered. That case will be considered in the forthcoming **FIP** publication, **Forensic Pathology: Next Time The Fire**.

routinely thinking first of that and he and I talked frequently about contact points, which was a concept that what you're actually trying to do in forensic science is that you're trying to work out what the contact points are between the offender and the victim, the offender and the scene because that is where the transfer evidence will be and the victim and the scene and you could only really do that by working out the whole of the sequence of events, round about the time of death. You could call it the micro-sequence of events".

Barclay gives an example of the type of thinking that modern pathologists will take into account. "For example—a really obvious example—if a girl has been attacked and somebody wants to force her to have oral sex—so it's a sexually motivated homicide—but it all goes wrong and she's murdered, then you need to work out in ten years time where you're likely to get evidence of contact between the offender and the victim", Barclay said. "And if he hasn't succeeded in having sex with her or oral sex with her, then it's not going to be the swabs, but if you think of yourself trying to control a girl's head, because you want to control her and she's got a pony tail, your contact point is the pony tail. Most girls will wear a scrunchy or something like that, so that scrunchy definitely contains DNA of the offender and it's probably been put in a bag ten years earlier and the DNA in that is going to be as good now as it was at the time. Nobody's messed with it because nobody's thought of it. It's only when you look at the sequence of events—the micro-sequence of events that you see the significance of that pony tail and the significance of the scrunchy".

So, detecting and preserving the integrity of contact points are of vital importance. Consequently, overturning the primacy of forensic pathologists and integrating the discipline into the needs of modern investigative techniques was essential.

CHAPTER 38

Teamwork

The New Order

While it may be excusable that nobody thought of the scrunchy ten years ago, it isn't anymore. It is vital evidence, but before they could get such thinking to be common-place, changes were required in the mind-sets. "Now, a pathologist is in a very good position to do that if he's got an investigative hat on — if he thinks he's part of a team which is trying to do that sort of thing — and there was general unease in the detective training at that time that that was not always the case", Barclay said referring to the scrunchies. "I was responsible for lecturing at Bramshill to senior courses in detective training, major incident, 'Management of Serious Series Crime' and so on and there was pretty well general unease that the pathologists turned up and did their thing and then went away again and often it was maybe two or three weeks before you got the report, because they didn't want to commit themselves until they'd done histology or whatever".

The delays were infuriating to police. "But what the SIO wanted to know was what was their first impressions, what they thought had happened and so on", Barclay explained. "There were also some incidents in London round about that time which were clearly wrong. Gary Pugh, round about that time, 2004–05, was the Head of Scientific Services for the Met. He, and myself, and a retired senior detective from South Yorkshire, Mick Burdiss, formed a group of three people to design a new system for the relationship between the SIOs, Home Office and pathologists".

It was the beginning of the end of the old order.

Team Ethic

"One of the problems with forensic pathology was that not only didn't they see themselves as part of a team, but many of them saw themselves as a sole practitioner", Barclay said. "They were the only person that was doing it and they sometimes got defensive if somebody criticised them, because most of the time the only time they were criticised was in court by a pathologist working for the defence. What should have happened is that somebody should have raised those issues with them before the report was actually finalised. They could have come together and actually agreed, 'Oh well actually, another explanation for it might be this, whatever', so if they hadn't thought of it, they got defensive when they went to court. They should have been in a little group like every other profession I think—certainly like forensic scientists—and yeah, like every other group, I think. Even the police have got reviews, you know, mandatory reviews after 28 days and after three months of unsolved cases, but the pathologists didn't".

And so the changes were rung in. It had taken far too long, but finally forensic pathology had been unified across the UK as part of the investigative team. "In pathology they now have to work in a group practice of at least three, so they had to form themselves into group practices whether they liked it or not and some of them didn't like it and the further north they went the less they liked it", Barclay said. "All your work has got to be peer-reviewed. It's got to be counter-signed by a colleague—normally within your group of three—but all the reports are put on a National Database, which is restricted to forensic pathologists, and they're accessible to all the other forensic pathologists, so they can be read and are read by everybody, but only by a forensic pathologist".

Peer-review

As with other forensic science disciplines, forensic pathologists now had to submit their work to peer-review. It was an important safeguard, but was it independent? After all, it was conducted by their closest colleagues. Would that not put pressure on the peer-reviewer, and what if you had a maverick who chose to avoid it in order to put some outlandish hypothesis forward, or some cock-up occurred? What if it was not verified as peer-reviewed by the paperwork being counter-signed as had occurred in the Lynette White Inquiry? What consequences should that incur? Whether it was peer-reviewed or not, Dr Whiteside offered an opinion in evidence that the science and other evidence did not support. Despite the flaws in peer-reviewing in that case, Barclay still thinks that colleagues would raise criticisms in peer-review.

"I still think they might have done", Barclay says. "They would have different deficiencies. Was it deficiency that they couldn't be bothered, or was it deficiencies that they had weak spots about shaken baby syndrome or whatever and if it was the latter, if it was a matter of technique, they would have raised it with each other? Even so, putting people in a group of three, that's very difficult to say that it must be effective on its own. It can't be just that group of three, but people can look at the reports and as far as I know many of the complaints about the various pathologists who have been disciplined actually came from within the forensic pathology system. There was no difficulty in finding other pathologists to say that they weren't performing well".

And so a form of accountability was introduced to forensic pathology and formalised. Time will tell how effective it is, but Barclay believes it is a step in the right direction. "I should say that major change is not so much the peer-review, because many pathologists were doing it anyway, or some of the better pathologists were doing it as a matter of course, because I think they're taught that anyway when they're doctors — e.g. on ward rounds", Barclay says. "You have to justify your actions, but it's saying to them up front and it does say to them up front, 'you are part of the investigative team, the same as a forensic scientist'. There is no primacy and in the past many pathologists felt they had primacy and I've seen some super examples of that".

CHAPTER 39

Interpretations

Procedures

The Dutch DNA expert—currently based in the USA—Richard Eikelenboom, explains the importance of his work with reference to the high profile Schiedammer Park attacks. In the summer of 2000, ten year-old Nienke Kleiss went to the Beatrix Park in the village of Schiedam in the Netherlands with her eleven year-old friend Maikel Willebrand. They were viciously attacked by Wik Haalmeijer. Kleiss tried to fight Haalmeijer off, but died in the attempt. Willebrand's quick wits saved his life—he played dead. Eikelenboom was the DNA expert who devised the protocols based on those used by the FSS for Low Template or Low Copy Number (LCN) DNA. Eikelenboom had to identify the contact points—the areas that the perpetrator had to have touched while committing the crimes. These were the locations where he would look for DNA to amplify.

Eikelenboom knew that because there were two victims that involved separate contact points and that the DNA of the perpetrator would be at those contact points too, but that there would be mixtures too. Despite the difficulties, Eikelenboom realised that there was a real prospect of obtaining useful DNA that could help to convict the perpetrator. Artefacts could be a problem too, but Eikelenboom explained why in general artefacts should not pose such a big problem (see below). He worked out where useful DNA was likely to be located and took samples from those locations at the crime-scene. These included on Kleiss' fingernails, her bare belly and her bare shoulder, although there were other locations which were important too. The most important were from the bootlaces of Willebrand, which were used to strangle both Kleiss and Willebrand. All of the locations should have been disclosed to the defence of the man who wrongly stood trial for these crimes, Kees Borsboom, but they were not. This caused the Schiedammer Park Inquiry to go awry. The interpretation of the results played an important part in the miscarriage of justice that followed as well.

Importance and Interpretation

LCN helped to resolve the notorious Schiedammer Park crimes—small quantities were involved as this was touch DNA. "At that time what we did was look at all the profiles and see which are not stutter artefacts and match or do not match our two victims, because then we are looking at someone who could be the perpetrator", Eikelenboom explained. "I took his sample at three locations—actually I took them at ten—but three on the shoe-lace. I got DNA not matching the two victims and I would think, 'Well that could be coming from the perpetrator, because why would an unknown male (not being the father or mother, or other person) touch the shoe-lace of this boy, exactly at the locations where the perpetrator touched it?' It's not very likely, so we thought, let's have a look at the locations where we found common alleles, not matching the two victims".

Eikelenboom had found DNA that did not come from either victim at crucial locations in the crime-scene—the importance of these results was obvious. It was clear that they had the DNA of the perpetrator, but as with other cases, a simple situation became complicated as the wrong man had been arrested and charged—Borsboom was not the source of those alleles. He should have been eliminated, but that did not happen. The simple and correct explanation was ignored in favour of a fanciful one that contributed to a miscarriage of justice once a confession—an erroneous one—had been obtained. Borsboom retracted it, but it counted for nothing. Partial disclosure also ambushed the defence and contributed to a gross miscarriage of justice which the forensic science could and should have prevented, but like the Lynette White Inquiry it was not allowed to speak freely and truly. Kees Borsboom and the reputation of Dutch justice paid the price.

Spurious Explanations

Eikelenboom explained the results that he found at particular genes (loci) and their significance. DNA was located on a number of areas on Nienke Kleiss, some of which were plainly significant. Kleiss bit her nails. They were short. She had been swimming with Willebrand shortly before they were viciously attacked by Haalmeijer. That meant that the DNA on her nails had been shed by someone she had contact with after going swimming. Obviously this was the DNA of the perpetrator, as he was the only source of foreign DNA that she came into contact with after her swim. It was plainly significant.

The selective disclosure of some of the results and locations from which they were obtained allowed the Dutch authorities to ensure that the significance of Eikelenboom's results were misinterpreted. It was suggested that the disclosed results had been deposited by a school-friend—a convenient explanation as the only means of eliminating the possibility would have been to DNA test several children, and that was never going to have been allowed. DNA was found on her belly, shoulder, nails, the boot-lace and boots too. The same alleles which did not belong to either victim or their families were found at all these locations—it would have been an incredible coincidence if all of these alleles just happened to have been deposited by a school-mate at precisely the positions the perpetrator would have been expected to shed his. They had to be those of the perpetrator. That enabled Eikelenboom to deduce the contribution donated by the perpetrator and eliminate anyone who did not possess those alleles.[1]

"It looks like the perpetrator has a 13 [at locus D8], because all the locations together", he explained. "It is very, very unusual that this would be a coincidence that an unknown person has a certain hair, so we are certain already that this is some information that we are looking at the same person. [It is the] Same as the hair at VWA and left boot of Nienke, left shoulder and left boot of victim, so not the boot of the boy. There are finger-scrapings and the three locations on the shoe-lace. Of course, everywhere there is two victims not one sample where there is not DNA of two victims—so we have DNA of at least three persons. So we have six times on boot and three times on left shoelace. These we found on all locations. We checked around 2000 people—no [full] hits. We got 80 hits actually, but when we look at the profile manually, you can see if someone is matching or not".

These DNA results should have ensured that the miscarriage of justice that followed could not have happened. Borsboom did not possess these

1. Any difference in alleles was enough to eliminate, even if some matched.

alleles. He should have been eliminated, but selective disclosure of locations and results allowed a false explanation to be given. It was claimed that the DNA had probably been shed by school-friends. It was untrue and obviously so, as it could not explain the foreign alleles at all the locations that Eikelenboom mentioned. Haalmeijer possessed all the foreign alleles — Borsboom did not. Reporting Officer, Ate Kloostermann, later claimed that he had disclosed that there were other DNA results. He had, but he knew or certainly should have known, that the locations and the subsequent interpretation of its meaning were vitally important. Haalmeijer's guilt was eventually proved when he was arrested on unrelated crimes and insisted on DNA testing to support his unsolicited confession to the Schiedammer Park crimes.

Complicated

The case was made complicated when it should not have been. Eikelenboom had found very useful information — evidence that could and should have prevented a miscarriage of justice and would have if the defence had been supplied with the information that they needed. It was information that Kloostermann and the prosecution knew Borsboom's defence had a right to it. If the full results and their significance had been disclosed, it would have been obvious that the perpetrator was not Borsboom. There were further complications caused by poor crime-scene practices too. Despite the advice of the pathologist, evidential items were put in the same body bag as a strangled victim and removed from the scene. That destroyed DNA evidence as fluids were released from the body, which contaminated any of the DNA on the boots. That may well have contained the DNA of the perpetrator, but putting those items in the same body bag as a victim of homicide who had been strangled, destroyed it as evidence. Such lax procedures cannot be acceptable in this day and age.

While artefacts may not be significant for the reasons referred to below, the protocols developed by Eikelenboom are very important for many reasons. Not only can they prevent miscarriages of justice, but also they were essential to tie Haalmeijer to his crimes in Schiedammer Park and prove the innocence of Borsboom and also Willebrand — the first and most absurd of those suspected. Willebrand was a child — not even in his teens.

Artefacts

Another issue that has to be considered in modern investigations is the effect of artefacts, although while it is a technical issue, it is not really as complicated as it seems. Depending on the number of amplification cycles conducted, there is a risk of artefacts being created—they are spurious peaks that have nothing to do with the DNA being tested. "That's quite a technical story", he says. Eikelenboom provided a demonstration and explains why artefacts are not as significant as may appear at first glance with reference to the Schiedammer Park case. Eikelenboom explained why with the aid of a profile showing the size and location of peaks. It would require a remarkable coincidence for an artefact to be significant in any case. It would have to appear at precisely the same allele position as that of the person of interest. It's not really likely, but it is 'technically possible'. Eikelenboom explains the issues regarding artefacts.

"They are always around very high peaks", he said. "6000 is very high peak, so they are either in front of it or one at the back, but like with this one, this is the high peak. It's 4000 [shows the peaks]. There are more than three alleles in between. It is very unlikely this one is an artefact, because they always exist or come to exist because of the high peaks. The high peaks do not always get very well amplified and if you know about amplification, we amplify all DNA. Sometimes something is breaking off. If something is breaking off, because that's the most common artefacts, you get a small easy peak—a very small peak in front of the high peak. If you have loads of copies of course something goes wrong because you have genetic things and sometimes something is not amplified correctly. Normally, you start measuring it if you have this huge amount of DNA and of course the amplification mistakes also take place if you amplify with more cycles, so the most common artefacts for LCN DNA is stutter artefacts. They can be in front, but sometimes they can also be in the back, so you have to be careful with the ones in the front with the high peaks and in the back more. It is complicated".

Nevertheless, it is possible to identify which are likely to be artefacts—Eikelenboom's point—and consequently eliminate their potential effect from scientific investigations.

CHAPTER 40

Solutions

Expertise

There is no doubt that properly constituted forensic science has a very important role to play in preventing injustice and also helping to deliver justice. It can and must serve those high ideals. The former FSR, Andrew Rennison, believes that it must benefit the courts to deliver justice. "I step right outside of my area of accreditation and expertise, but I'd like to give a personal view on this", Rennison said after hearing details of a scandalous injustice in South Africa — the Eikenhof Three. "All expert evidence, and I include forensic science in that, is there for the benefit of the court, not for any particular party in a case, so I want to get forensic science in a position where it's helping the courts on every occasion to reach the right decision and I've already published a paper which sets out the legal responsibilities of an expert witness on my website, because there is no doubt that the duties of an expert witness in the criminal justice system are onerous and described as such by Sir Anthony Campbell in his review of the Scottish fingerprint inquiry. He said of all levels of forensic science, the experts then give the evidence — have a very onerous duty — and their duty is not to support the case for the people who are instructing and paying them, it is to be totally objective and true with their evidence for the benefit of the court".

Rennison's view, which we support, is that forensic science has no side and nor should forensic scientists. The evidence must be allowed to speak freely. Sadly, this is an issue in many jurisdictions. The case of the Eikenhof Three is such a case. It was a plainly preventable injustice, caused in part by a corrupt criminal justice system that was part and parcel of a crime against humanity, apartheid. It was obvious from an early stage that the Eikenhof attack on a car carrying five white people, was ordered by and executed by the Azanian People's Liberation Army (APLA), the armed wing of the Pan-Africanist Congress of Azania (PAC).

However, corrupt policing and political expediency conspired to place three African National Congress (ANC) members in the sights of the Apartheid state.[1] This case illustrates much that is wrong throughout the criminal justice system of South Africa at that time. The truth began to emerge when the commander of the APLA cell, Phila Dolo, applied for amnesty to the Truth and Reconciliation Commission (TRC) in 1997. The weapons used in the other attack—the one he was imprisoned for—was linked through forensic science to the Eikenhof attack. Despite this and more, it took a further two years for the Eikenhof Three to be released. This was an example of justice delayed even after the forensic science had made its contribution.

Perceptions

"I think what you've just described are examples where expert evidence is allowed to be skewed in a particular direction to suit a particular argument, not to help the court reach a fair and just decision", Rennison said. "Under varying jurisdictions, but certainly here in the UK—sorry England and Wales the criminal procedure rules are absolutely fundamentally clear that the forensic science expert is there to help the court and is not there to support a particular side. The problem is our system of justice doesn't necessarily allow that to happen, so the accusatorial system naturally ends up pitting experts against each other".

This results in the inevitable 'guns for hire' problem as experts are seen as leaning towards giving evidence that meets the requirements of the side that instructed them, whether that is true or not. Rennison is certainly aware of this perception and has tackled it.

1. ANC members Siphiwe Bholo, Zipho Gavin and Titi 'Boy' Ndweni suffered an appalling miscarriage of justice in South Africa as Apartheid was in its death throes. They were wrongfully convicted of the murder of Zandra Mitchley, Shaun Nel and Claire Silberbauer and the attempted murder of Craig Lamprecht and Norman Mitchley, whose car was attacked in Eikenhof in 1993. The car was shot at causing the deaths and injuries. The truth emerged during the Truth and Reconciliation Commission hearings. This included the weapons used being linked to the APLA unit and that they had been used in other operations. The Eikenhof Three were freed in November 1999 by order of Transvaal Deputy Judge President, Edward Stafford. A retrial ordered by the appeal court never occurred. Consequently, they have not received the exoneration and vindication that they deserve. The Eikenhof attack was an operation by the APLA. It is important to note that this was a case where an integrated and honest approach to the investigation would have prevented a grave miscarriage of justice. Forensic science could have played a part too.

"The perception is that they have loyalty to the side that they're working for", Rennison says. "What happens in reality is that if the case is managed properly and the criminal procedure rules are applied properly, the judges will insist that the two experts are brought together in a very early case conference where they discuss their differences and their agreements and what tends to happen is that the stories then leads to an impact of competing against each other in the witness box, [but] when they meet face to face and have a sensible scientific based discussion, most end up in agreement".

Nevertheless, consensus does not always occur, but it could and should occur in most cases as the science ought to be clear, meaning that controversy should not surface, or should only do so rarely, as the science itself should not be in dispute. There may, however, be disagreement over interpretation of results. "The disagreements disappear", Rennison said. "They [the 'opposing' scientists] meet in the middle with very solid middle-ground. The courts find that really, really helpful and it provides very objective evidence, so I would like to see forensic science very properly case-managed through the court process, so that experts are allowed to deliver the area of dispute to a court, which provides much, much more objective evidence. It is healthy".

According to Rennison, judges will accept that experts could disagree over what has happened and the significance of it if there is a problem with the administration of criminal process rules and that such disagreement may not have been over a sinister occurrence. So, procedures are now in place to develop consensus between experts wherever possible. Peer-review will reduce conflict of opinion too, although interpretation — whether disagreement is honest or not — may remain a thorny issue.

Advances

Advances in various forensic sciences have rendered some of the problems of the past obsolete. Nevertheless, it has to be remembered that the safeguard of peer-review existed in the Lynette White Inquiry, yet despite the very clear picture that the forensic science and crime-scene were trying to tell, an utterly distorted one was allowed to be presented and result in a notorious miscarriage of justice. That happened with the safeguard of peer-review in place, because for some reason either it failed to occur as required, or it failed to prevent an erroneous hypothesis from being put forward as evidence. It remains to be seen how the methods described prevent a repetition of what happened in the Lynette White Inquiry, for example. Nevertheless, Rennison believes that the errors of the past, such as those that occurred in the Lynette White Inquiry, will not recur because of the new procedures.

"Forensic science has moved on considerably since then [the early 1990s] as have police investigation methodologies and so the forensic science methods employed back in this era are completely different to those employed now, because the technology's moved on significantly", Rennison said. "You'll find that in an inquiry like this [the Lynette White Inquiry] nowadays, the first method that will be routinely employed is DNA technology and it would have resolved this case very, very quickly, so we are seeing inquiries such as this resolved far quicker nowadays with far quicker results produced through DNA technology and over the last decade DNA technology has improved considerably and is about to go through the next sea change from 10 loci through to 15 loci and new multiplex kits coming on the market, which will remove even further some of the issues, which we've had with the SGM+ kits."

Rennison is right—partly. DNA was in its infancy at the time, but it should still have prevented the injustice that occurred. While Dr Nicholas Prance was absolutely correct in his opinion that degradation and the treatment of the samples with the fingerprinting chemical ninhydrin could cause a band to shift out of position,[2] the conventional methods used by Professor Barclay could have answered those questions anyway. It was unfortunately another example of a closed mind in the investigation

2. The significance of this was that in 1989 the Cardiff Five had been eliminated as the source of blood on two wallpaper samples. Others including the prime suspect, whom the author refers to as Mr X in his book **Fitted In: The Cardiff and the Lynette White Inquiry**, were excluded on this basis. If it had been Lynette's blood then it was not just the DNA eliminations of the Cardiff Five that could not be relied on, but everyone, including Mr X. However, the methods used by Professor Barclay in his review could and should have been used to identify whether those samples which were referred to as SS2 and SS12 were likely to have been shed by Lynette or the killer. More sophisticated DNA testing would resolve this once and for all during the Phase II investigation that identified Jeffrey Gafoor as the real killer of Lynette White.

and prosecution. Would the question have even been asked of Prance if the DNA results had not been so inconvenient to the case against the Cardiff Five? This was yet another example of forensic science being seen as serving the interests of a particular side. However, the advances in DNA testing systems means that blood grouping evidence will never be capable of such misinterpretation as occurred in the Lynette White Inquiry again for the reasons Rennison mentions.

As Rennison points out, the new system will be more discriminating too — all of which will help to prevent the scope for such injustices to occur. It will offer a random match statistic greater than the population on of the world. "It hasn't got a name in the way that SGM+ has, but it's 15 loci as opposed to 10, so it's far more discriminating", said Rennison. "It is far better able to deal with inhibition, which is something you do raise in your book, because inhibition can affect the quality of the profile, so, for example, denim is a material that can inhibit the quality, so it's been proven to be able to manage the effects of inhibition. It will reduce the need to, in every case, measure the quantity of DNA that's there, because it can routinely manage with very, very low quantities of DNA, so it will be removing the distinction between Low Templates and ordinary DNA technologies because this will just cover the whole lot, so I think the short answer is that we're in a very different world now".

And this is the world that forensic pathology has to be integrated into.

CHAPTER 41

Quality Control

The Groundwork

The former Forensic Science Regulator, Andrew Reninson, had explained why he believes that the problems that plagued previous cases, such as the Lynette White Inquiry, would not occur now. The science has advanced to the point of making the method used then—blood grouping—all but obsolete. In Phase II of the Lynette White Inquiry more sophisticated DNA testing not only proved who the source of the relevant blood staining was, but equally importantly, who it was not. Nevertheless, the quality controls that were in place even in 1989, such as peer-review, should have weeded out the scientifically ludicrous cocktail-hypothesis before it wreaked the havoc that it did with the interests of justice. That did not happen. Although some FSS scientists, such as Trevor Howitt, Nicholas Prance and Peter Gill raised concerns over Whiteside's work, this happened behind closed doors and did not stop Whiteside giving evidence that implied the cocktail-hypothesis was the most viable explanation for the foreign blood staining, when it plainly was not.

The quality control mechanisms have improved since then, but it cannot be denied that there were quality control measures in place and they simply failed to work in this case. This has never been fully accounted for. Advances in quality control notwithstanding, this cannot be permitted to occur again and that cannot happen without thorough review of what happened. None of the previous reviews have addressed this. Consequently, I raised concerns over the way the forensic science evidence was presented in this case.[1] It was considered by Stephen Carey,

1. These concerns were first raised in my book **Fitted In: The Cardiff 3 and the Lynette White Inquiry**. I expanded on them in my second book **The Cardiff Five: Innocent Beyond Any Doubt**. Furthermore, I was asked to detail my concerns about Dr Whiteside's work for the Phase III investigation by Detective Superintendent John Penhale. I did so in August 2005. This resulted in Professor Barclay's review of Whiteside's cocktail-hypothesis and the comments that I had made about it at that time.

a consultant Senior Investigating Officer, who was previously a Detective Superintendent and Head of the Major Crime Branch of Devon and Cornwall Police. His brief was to determine whether the Phase III investigation was fit for purpose regarding its enquiries about Whiteside. It looked at further issues relating to Whiteside as well, but it was limited in its scope. It was concerned with the effect on policing — my concerns are wider. This is a classic example of the need for an integrated approach between policing, the forensic sciences and judicial processes too. The repeated failure to get to the full truth in this case, illustrated by the failure to establish if Whiteside's statements had even been peer-reviewed as required, clearly demonstrates the overwhelming need for a Truth and Justice Commission into the whole of this wretched case — the lessons must be learned before the errors are repeated.

Changing Attitudes

Rennison detailed the quality controls measures that had been introduced in Britain by the FSS since the ill-fated Lynette White Inquiry resulted in a notorious miscarriage of justice — controls that forensic pathology had to be brought into line with. "The Forensic Science Service began a huge project which they kicked off in 1991", Rennison explained. "They invested £2m in early accreditation. That project from 1991 had a huge impact in changing attitudes within the Forensic Science Service, whereby the organisation became far more accountable for the quality of the work it started delivering. It brought in very robust quality management systems, which should prevent that sort of lone ranger type work happening again and so they brought in proper peer-reviewing, quality management, proficiency testing, deep sampling, security checks — good basic quality management stuff. Here the FSS became good at that".

In fact, the FSS had quality management systems previously and they were usually effective. An example of those systems of quality assurance and quality control that were operational throughout the 80s included blind and open trials co-ordinated via the FSS laboratory at Aldermaston. However, the police only became aware of it when the FSS became an Agency in 1991 and defence lawyers, found out about it even later, if at all. The project that Rennison referred to brought in accreditation of the laboratories via NAMAs and ISO 9001. But peer-reviewing at least had been established in FSS laboratories far earlier, although as the Lynette White Inquiry showed, the lack of consequences for apparent failure to comply demonstrated that it was not fool-proof.[2] Nevertheless, attitudes had begun to change and the FSS, much maligned over high profile failures, played a major role in driving up standards of management and quality control as Rennison explains.

"They have exported that methodology across Europe and the guy that led all this is Dr Bob Bramley, the chief scientist", Rennison said. "He did a fantastic job. He chaired the Quality Confidence Committee in the European Network of Forensic Science Institutes. Over the following ten years we helped drive this proper course of management approach across Europe—no globally—so there's a huge change of attitude. It wasn't helped I don't think by decisions made in the late 1990s–1998 to go for a Register of Forensic Practitioners. So the government was concerned about quality failings, which was largely one-sided on what the FSS did to drive up quality management systems".

Further Problems

Nevertheless, any system can only be as efficient as the zeal with which it is enforced, especially when the procedures are not followed rigorously. For the system that Rennison described to achieve its potential, organisations have to take responsibility for their staff and work together with other relevant organisations. There were false starts and exclusive approaches to the problem as Rennison explains: "The police of course didn't come up with any of that", he said. "They carried on doing their own thing, so in 1998 the government sanctioned the birth of the Council for Registration of Forensic Practitioners, which fell into exactly the same trap in that it put the focus right back on individual practitioners and not on the organisation. So it tried to regulate the individuals, but I think it missed the point and the organisations then, senior Chief Executives and Chief Constables weren't accountable enough".

---

2. For further information see my third book **Trials and Tribulations—Innocence Matters?** which was published by **The Fitted-In Project** in 2017.

Rennison has a valid point. Time was lost, but eventually it was put back on track. "Well we changed all of that and we shifted accountability right back onto the organisations", Rennison said. "So some of the things you say shouldn't happen [any more], because you have quality checks all the way through the process now, but there's still a lot of work to be done to get that to work in the way I want it".

Duties

One problem, which hopefully will not happen again, is the failure of existing safeguards that occurred in the Lynette White Inquiry. It also illustrates Rennison's views, as the FSS did not deliver organisational responsibility either. There is no evidence that Whiteside's controversial cocktail-hypothesis was peer-reviewed, but that indicates an organisational failing. The original investigation was essentially saying correctly that the evidence indicated that the killer was one person acting on their own and that person was a male. Then things got skewed by the discovery of Angela Psaila's blood groups. She did not volunteer that she was there and participated in the murder. She denied and protested and protested and denied until her will was overborne. After police were informed about her blood groups she was told that her blood had been discovered in the flat and that that proved that she had been there. It was not true, but she was persuaded of it. That could not have happened without Whiteside telling them that Psaila's combination of blood groups was significant. It plainly was not as other evidence showed—evidence that Whiteside was fully aware of.

Other FSS scientists raised concerns about aspects of Whiteside's work, which suggests that some organisational responsibility was taken, but this failed to prevent an incredible hypothesis from skewing the thinking to the point that it aided and abetted a miscarriage of justice in the making—one that subsequently happened. Forensic science should never be used and abused in that manner and no provider of forensic sciences should allow their organisation to be brought into disrepute in that manner. The FSS should have ensured that its procedures were followed to the letter. Plainly, that didn't happen in this case and if it could happen in a high profile case like this, how many other cases could similar failings have happened in — ones denied the glare of publicity that this had? Whiteside's statements should have been counter-signed if they had been peer-reviewed. In this case, that cannot be said. His employers, the FSS, should have ensured that he complied with their own requirement that his work was peer-reviewed and that the paperwork was up to the required standard. There should have been no doubt. The counter-signature would have removed all doubt. The FSS owed a duty of care to guarantee that its own procedures had been properly followed. They did not meet that duty. That was a serious organisational failing.

"It becomes a complete prophecy in effect — a self-fulfilling theory — doesn't it?" Rennison said. "Well good practice in forensic science nowadays is to have all your work peer-reviewed".

So what would have happened if it had definitely been peer-reviewed?

"Difficult to give a definitive answer", Rennison said. "I would sincerely hope that it would not have passed. You go back to square one and you re-evaluate all the forensic evidence and you advise the investigating team accordingly".

But safeguards can only be as effective as the zeal with which they are enforced, and in this case they were found to be sadly lacking more than once.

CHAPTER 42

Zeal

Decision-making

To be effective, safeguards must be enforced and the zeal with which they are enforced is the true test of how effective they are in practice. Whiteside's work should have been peer-reviewed at least once, and possibly twice — once for each statement that he made after the arrest of the Cardiff Five. Rennison was surprised. "Every time you start reaching conclusions when you're writing a report there should be a peer-review of that process and in this day and age there's much, much better note-taking, so other people can see exactly how your decision-making's working, [and] how you reached those conclusions", Rennison said. "And then the FSS went through a huge programme. It's all about how you interpret and present evidence — huge shift in culture, so the way that case was handled wouldn't happen now. What I set out to do was reinforce through accreditation not just a peer-review in each case but a peer-review of all the processes in your laboratory to make sure they are robust and rational and working".

It is also a pity that Professor Barclay's work on the Lynette White Inquiry has not been published, and nor has the review conducted by the then senior FSS scientist Alistair McPhee. Consequently, no explanation has been given as to how peer-review, if it occurred, failed to function effectively and what needs to be done about it now to ensure that repetition cannot occur. Perhaps the FSR could take it on?

"I have to be very guarded", Rennison said. "If I start taking on that sort of work, I would sink very quickly. I am running a number of what I would describe as complaints where there have been problems in forensic science laboratories and we do where we can. We go in and look and we publish the case — what I have described. It's fundamentally an issue of resources. I am not resourced. An inquiry into a case like the Lynette White case would take considerable effort on my part, because to do it properly, I'd have to go back through all the historical records, speak to people and form my own conclusions. That would be a huge amount of work. *I think there's a good argument for doing it.* I am quite simply not resourced and able to do that, where organisations like the IPCC[1] and others probably are, but it's me and three or four people. Maybe the IPCC should be considering a similar approach and should be taking more. Maybe they do take advice from other forensic scientists. I don't know, but they don't come to me. They are welcome to" [my emphasis].

Then Who?

It appears that the FSR could not review individual cases, however important they are, and Rennison agreed that this plainly was and is an important case. The safeguard of peer-review failed to function as intended, but despite that failure, which may have been caused by deliberate evasion, alarm bells did not ring at the time, or even subsequently. In 1995 the then Home Secretary, Michael Howard, was invited to order a public inquiry into cases in South Wales, but through his then junior ministers, Sir David MacLean and Ann Widdecombe, it was refused. The request for a public inquiry then was made by the author and a then Shadow Home Office Minister, Alun Michael, now the Police and Crime Commissioner for South Wales, partly due to concerns over failures in forensic science in these cases. An utterly inappropriate course of action suggested by those ministers made the problem worse. They insisted that I should take my concerns to the Chief Constable of South Wales Police, knowing full well that I had no reason to trust the then Chief Constable of South Wales, the late Robert Lawrence.[2] The inquiry was re-opened and controlled by Phil Jones, then Head of South Wales CID.

1. On January 8th 2018 the IPCC was replaced with the Independent Office for Police Conduct.
2. After the convictions of the Cardiff Three were quashed in December 1992, Lawrence robustly defended his force. An internal report by Assistant Chief Constable Bob Evans quickly concluded that South Wales Police had done nothing wrong. Knowing that this was Lawrence's opinion, MacLean and Widdecombe expected me to trust my concerns to a man who had demonstrated a lack of impartiality. They must have known that it would not happen and perhaps that was their intention. Then as now, I do not believe in self-regulation. And then there was Detective Chief Superintendent Phil Jones. Despite his acknowledgement that the Cardiff Five were innocent, I did not trust him. I would later be proved right as he was jailed for corruption. Such was the calibre of people the then government wanted to be trusted to investigate concerns over the integrity of high profile inquiries.

South Wales Police demanded that I give whatever evidence of police or other 'corruption' that I had to them. As I had no reason to trust them to investigate themselves or anyone else involved in that inquiry or other controversial investigations in that jurisdiction, I ignored their demands.

Consequently, concerns over Whiteside's conduct were not raised or investigated at a time when fuller records would have been available and memories less hazy. It should also be noted that Whiteside threatened legal action against me — proceedings that never occurred over strong criticisms that I made of his cocktail-hypothesis. Furthermore, Jones later became a private investigator and was jailed for corruption offences — he recruited former colleague David Lloyd, who was working for South Wales Police at the time, to access police computers to aid his private investigations. Judge Simon Darwall-Smith sentenced Jones to 18 months imprisonment in March 2010. "For a person of your age and former seniority, retiring at the rank of Detective Chief Superintendent, it saddens this court to see how you conspired with your friends David Lloyd and [Christopher] Barnett because you knew they were prepared to break the law to access information", Darwall-Smith said at the time. "This lack of moral fibre on your part goes to the root of the corrupt culture existing in parts of the force. The public would be justifiably outraged if you didn't receive an immediate custodial sentence".

Self-Regulation

This was the calibre of investigator that those former ministers thought should be trusted to investigate serious allegations of malpractice. Consequently, a golden opportunity to establish what had happened in the Lynette White Inquiry and how, was wasted. The blame for this rests squarely with the Conservative government that was in power at that time. Without such review, how can lessons be learned? Further opportunities were wasted. South Wales Police insisted on having the opportunity to put right what they had got wrong after the vindication of the Cardiff Five. It was a genuine attempt made by a force that had recognised at top level that it had a serious institutional problem that had to be corrected, but ultimately a flawed one — one that failed in a climate of secrecy where openness had been promised. Over a hundred recommendations were made by the Reviewing Officer Bill Hacking—not one has been published. Assurances that they have been implemented cannot be verified without knowing what they are. Not one of the three inquiries into the only aspect investigated—the collapsed trial—have published these recommendations. A promise to disclose the Hacking Report was reneged on in 2000 and again later. It has never been published. Consequently, it is unclear if it contained any criticism of Whiteside and the manipulation of what the forensic science was actually saying and if the recommendations included anything designed to prevent repetition of the use and abuse of the forensic science that occurred in this case.

Whiteside was one of 34 people arrested on suspicion of offences that included perjury and conspiracy to pervert the course of justice. He was later interviewed under caution in 14 tape-recorded interviews that occurred over two days with Professor Barclay officially 'downstream monitoring' the interviews—i.e. listening and suggesting questions to the police officers via a live link. The content of those interviews has never been revealed. Consequently, it is impossible to determine whether Whiteside provided adequate explanations for his conduct in this case. Whiteside was not prosecuted for his role in the Lynette White Inquiry. That decision was made by the CPS, which has not explained itself. The HMCPSI report into the failed prosecution does not explain it either and nor does the IPCC report. This is a matter of public importance, yet the CPS has not explained why he was not prosecuted. Was there not sufficient evidence? Was it not in the public interest? Why exactly was Whiteside spared prosecution? We still await an answer. The truth could have been established twenty years ago, but the Home Office Ministers chose to insist on the most inappropriate course possible—the consequences of that decision are still having an impact today. Despite this, successive governments have failed to deliver justice or learn the lessons, culminating in Theresa May's stubborn refusal to order an enquiry that could actually establish how and why a clear scientific picture was distorted beyond recognition and why there have been no consequences for such manipulation of the forensic science.

The Last Review?

Nevertheless, Rennison points out that it has been reviewed. Professor Barclay conducted a review. "Well there has been a reinvestigation of the case", Rennison said. "Your book's been published. There have been people like Barclay — David Barclay — poring over it, giving their views on it. He's done some fantastic work on it, so he's done a very thorough review of the forensic science in the original investigation and supported the reinvestigation, so most of that has been done. It's now how it's managed and dealt with".

While that is true, the facts established by Barclay have never been published. It is therefore impossible to establish exactly what went wrong and whether the flaws that contributed to a gross miscarriage of justice have been redressed. It needs thorough review, but the findings must be made public — there can be no enquiries conducted behind closed doors and reports that gather dust until they are archived and cannot serve the purpose their potential justifies.

Rennison has a suggestion and explanation.

"The Lynette White case is a very good example where I had discussions", Rennison said. "In fact, I did raise it with the Science and Technology Committee. If you look at the four movements of forensic science evidence throughout a case, there's a lot of activity by the police and other forensic scientists. Then it gets moved down the stream. Then problems start emerging and things go wrong. You are highly critical in some of your articles about bad lawyering and defence tactics and prosecution tactics and that has a huge influence on the outcome of a case. We know that. That's the system we have subscribed to. That could end up in a case collapsing. It could end up in a miscarriage of justice. It could end up in the CPS withdrawing a case. If this happens, you very rarely get any feedback on that outcome and there's very rarely a review on where it went wrong. My submission to the Science and Technology Committee asked the question: is there a role for the National Audit Office [NAO] to step in and do that?"

To date, that has not occurred. It is not the only part of the process that the NAO should consider.

Responsibilities

Fiscal responsibilities were also a consideration that affected the pace of change. "People are working hard to achieve results upstream", Rennison said. "They're working very hard at hugely reduced costs. There is no such impact downstream, because that's not their problem. Their problem's up here. They save their money. They've achieved their clear-up so they've got the tick in their performance box—someone is charged. They're not interested in the implications further downstream. What I see is, and the Lynette White case is a very good example of that, is the absence of any proper feedback put back to people. 'Well if you'd done this differently, the outcome would have been different'. Now, there's a number of players in that that could influence the outcome, so it could be that feedback has to go to the initial prosecuting lawyer. It could be the feedback goes to the case management strategist, the QC, wherever, but I don't see enough evidence of those feedback loops, so the people driving it upstream never really get at the issues downstream that they should be learning the lessons from, so it requires hard work".

Rennison at least saw the need to address the effects downstream. "I'm going to do a vertical audit now—the number of live cases to see if there are better ways of doing this and I have recommended considering that the National Audit Office do that as well, because that's a job they are very good at", he said. "It's full of value across the system, so where you've got people that think they've got value, they trim the costs down. They get in fast turn-around times. They're driving forensics very efficiently, very hard. Is there real value to the criminal justice system? You can always measure it".

But how do you measure it? And how do you account for the willingness to waste resources on deeply flawed processes that have yet to deliver justice, accountability, or even the truth while stubbornly refusing to initiate a process that would cost a fraction of the resources already wasted? Such a process would help to ensure that lessons are learned and that the modern investigative procedures that forensic pathology has been belatedly integrated into will not be compromised by preventable errors.

PART SEVEN

THE SAFEGUARDS

"There is no greater tyranny than that which is perpetrated under the shield of the law and in the name of justice".

Charles-Louis de Secondat, Baron de la Brède et de Montesquieu[1]

1. Montesquieu was an 18th-century French judge and philosopher (1689–1755). He is famed for advocating the separation of legal powers, see *The Spirit of Powers* (1748).

CHAPTER 43

Value

Measuring Value

It is obvious that nothing can expect a blank cheque, especially in the current economic climate, but the criminal justice system cannot be judged solely in fiscal terms. It must dispense justice without fear nor favour; and economic considerations should not determine access to justice, so how should value be gauged? It's a very important question — one that can't be ignored. It addresses the core issue: is there real value to the criminal justice system? The former Forensic Science Regulator, Andrew Rennison, thinks that it can be measured, but if so, how does he think that can be done?

"I'm going to go through some or all of this and I'm going to recruit some totally independent expert scientists to come and do that with me — probably put that out to tender", Rennison said. "We'll pick, or cherry pick a few very topical cases. We'll track them through the system and we'll look at the decision-making all the way down the line. Are there the right bridges of communication? Are the police not communicating properly with the forensic scientists? Are the scientists being told too much? Are the scientists being studious and not thinking of issues such as cognitive bias? We need to get a measure of this and then I think there is a role for the likes of the National Audit Office. We'll see where there are relations and what we can come up with".

This is an extremely important contribution, especially in the current economic debate, where paring to the bone seems to be the order of the day regardless of the impact on quality. Forensic science has a vital role to play in the delivery of justice, but while it cannot expect a blank cheque, it cannot deliver on fresh air either. Possible, or better still probable, outcomes need to be justified in advance of conducting particular tests, but never should the interests of justice be sacrificed for fiscal concerns. Justice is priceless — literally. It is people's lives that are at stake, after all. As long as a particular test or review can be justified as contributing to that, then it should be conducted, regardless of cost as its merit has been established. However, not liking a particular verdict or decision should never be grounds to conduct a test—it must address a core issue that affects the safety or potential safety of a conviction. However, if an injustice could have occurred, or be prevented, then erring should be on the side of prevention or cure.

It should also be noted that the Lynette White Inquiry, amongst others, is a classic example of the false economy approach that have dominated criminal justice system thinking. If the CPS and other parts of the criminal justice system had done their job efficiently in 1989 a fortune could have been saved, not to mention preventing the wrecking of many innocent lives. Despite recognition now of it being one of the most notorious miscarriages of justice in British history, the current government and its predecessor, were prepared to waste public funds on three inquiries into the same area, rather than on a process that would have cost a fraction, both in time and resources and delivered more—a Truth and Justice Commission into the whole case. Where is the fiscal responsibility that Rennison alluded to? Where is the justice in a process that cannot possibly get to the full truth because the enquiries that were set up were done so with limited terms of reference to not even look for it? It beggars belief that such an outdated and failed approach is being advanced again twenty years after the same approach was found wanting!

Quality and Expertise

But there are other important issues to consider, such as the quality of expertise available to both prosecution and defence. Rennison has tried to tackle this. "Going back four years ago now I nailed my colours very firmly to the work being done by the Law Commission on the reliability and admissibility of expert evidence, because I still firmly believe this", Rennison said. "I firmly believe that all parties in the process, particularly the courts should have clearer, probably more, powers to challenge or allow a challenge of expert evidence by other proper experts and to rule out the repeated problems we see with poor quality expertise. There is a general consensus out there now that expert evidence in the criminal justice system is often low grade, insufficiently challenged and doesn't go through enough checks and balances. The Law Commission I thought published some very good recommendations around all of that and those recommendations gathered dust in the Ministry of Justice. I'd like to see some action around those recommendations and I'd also point out that in discussions in front of the Science and Technology Committee, a lot of people have aired their concerns about defence access to good quality experts".

It was clear in the Lynette White Inquiry that expertise was an issue. One of the main things that went wrong was when the so-called cocktail-hypothesis was advanced by Dr Whiteside in court. Yusef Abdulahi's defence was looking for an expert to say that it was impossible. Neither John Hayward nor Patrick Lincoln would say that. The furthest they would go was that it was improbable, but it was more than scientifically improbable. Barclay demolished its credibility, using information and techniques that were available at the time because he assessed its likelihood in the actual context of the case. This begs the question of why the defence experts did not do likewise in 1989 or 1990. This is very strange, because it is a standard technique for defence counsel to try and 'deconstruct' scientific opinion based on several pieces of evidence in context. It is usually in their interests to try and downplay the significance of each scientific test by attacking them in isolation. This time the positions were reversed, or at least the Crown had to downplay the significance of certain results and the tests that produced them. The technically possible explanations outweighed the probable. Occam's Razor had rarely been so disregarded. Crown forensic scientists are taught not to allow this isolated approach in Court, and *never* to do it themselves — never to ignore one result in favour of another. But this is exactly what happened in the Lynette White trial. It was the prosecution which deconstructed the evidence to individual test results, and the defence scientists that for whatever reason did not take an overview of how likely all the results were, in the context of that particular crime. It should never have been allowed to happen. If the evidence that Barclay put forward in the Phase III investigation had been put forward at any time between the arrest of the Cardiff Five in 1988 and when the trials took place, it's quite likely the course of the case would have been different. There is no reason why this could not have been done when it could and should have made a real difference.

"Is that a consequence of the defence strategies — a consequence of failing to instruct the right expert?" Rennison asked when this was put to him. It was that but more — the wrong experts and the wrong expertise. It was neither a blood expert, nor a DNA expert that unravelled the mess. It was a review of what the evidence meant by a qualified scientist who had great experience of it. Had this been done in 1989 the outcome would almost certainly — bar a perverse verdict — have been different. But these are failings throughout the system. It was not just the original defence that needed such access to the relevant expertise, the police also needed it and the prosecution should have looked to test the hypothesis, because it was an obvious line of attack for the defence. That never happened. Instead bluff, bluster and obfuscation muddied what should have been a very clear scientific picture. There are lessons for forensic pathology and investigative processes in what happened in that case.

"After I gave my evidence, two people came to see me and said, 'We are for ever disillusioned with the general low calibre and poor quality of defence experts who are challenging cases'", Rennison said. "There is no regulation of that at all. It's outside my area of regulation, so we've got to give some serious thought to the scope of regulation here around who these people are and how far I reckon that because there's a growing concern that exactly in the Lynette White case, there isn't a robust enough review and defence of expert evidence that is put forward".

If only that had occurred in 1989, or even 1990. But these concerns are not limited to the Lynette White Inquiry. This is important in pathology too. The test of trial only works if the quality of expert meets the required standard to test the quality of the evidence. "Now one of the small but positive consequences of the closure of the Forensic Science Service is a huge increase in the availability of good quality science experts that are out there to defence teams", Rennison said. "So, they're becoming like principal forensic services, hearing about people who were the leading lights in the Forensic Science Service. They are now instructed more and more by defence and it's giving defence teams access to experts they never really had in the past. That's a good thing. We need to encourage more of that in the future".

But who regulates it?

CHAPTER 44

The Integrated Approach

The Need

Forensic pathology had to be brought into the modern era of investigative processes. Professor Dave Barclay's role in the Lynette White Inquiry was of great importance, but it would be an injustice to him not to acknowledge his role in helping to bring forensic pathology into the modern era, along with Mick Burdiss and Gary Pugh as well. The reasons why it had to be integrated into the investigative process were clear—the surprise was that it had taken so long. He explained the benefits of an integrated approach to crime-scene investigation in a still unsolved crime to illustrate the importance of this approach in modern investigations. "You've got a murder which happened in 1970 and it's a body found just off the M1",[1] Barclay said. "It's being reinvestigated by Derbyshire Police". This was a murder that could have benefited from the integrated approach that Barclay mentions back in 1970 when it occurred, but unfortunately it didn't get it then. The price of that remains high.

"We went to the scene and you have to go off the motorway to an exit, turn left, turn left again, over the motorway, up a steep hill and then take a sharp left up a track", Barclay explains as he builds up to the investigative point—an obvious but important one. "Imagine you're an offender; the track itself then goes steeply down, gets very wet at the bottom and that's where the body was deposited. As soon as you see that area and you look, well there are two things you see. You've actually gone back almost to the side of the motorway, so if you're a lorry driver, driving up and down the motorway, you can see where you dumped the body from

1. This is the unsolved murder of Barbara Mayo, which occurred on October 12th 1970. Her body was found at woods near Ault Hucknall in Derbyshire, across the fields from the M1. She had been raped, battered and strangled. DNA proved a link in 1990 between Mayo's murder, which was being investigated by Derbyshire Police, and the murder, also unsolved, of Jackie Ansell-Lamb who was sexually assaulted and murdered on March 8th 1970. Ansell-Lamb's murder was subsequently investigated by Cheshire Police, although that was not the case during the review that occurred in 1990.

the motorway, which is quite a strong psychological reason for doing it there—dumping the body there—but, you've now got your car or lorry at the bottom of a dip which is very wet with a steep slope up".

Barclay's points are salient. It is obvious that the perpetrator must have had considerable knowledge of the locality, and that should have been observed at the time. It should have helped focus lines of enquiry. Barclay emphasises the point. "You'd never ever go down that road in the car unless you knew that you could carry on and get out the other end", he said. "In fact you could go out through the woods about another half mile on and it comes out at a housing estate. The minute you look at that crime-scene 25 years later you know that person either lives locally, or has local knowledge because you would never have taken a car with someone you were going to kill or had killed already down that steep slope if you were going to get your car stuck at the bottom, so you know the person knows the locality.[2] Now that hadn't been appreciated at the time—hadn't been noticed at the time".

It is an astonishing omission—one that should not have been missed. This was vital information that may have helped unmask the killer back in 1970, as it could have helped police to focus attention on particular suspects and avoided wasting time on suspects who could have been eliminated for not having that local knowledge. But as Barclay acknowledges, attitudes have changed. "Nowadays we are far better at understanding crime-scenes and motivations, so working with pathologists, psychological profilers together gives us much more opportunity to get what I'm interested in which is physical evidence", he said.

Interpretation

Physical evidence is of great importance—even incomplete physical evidence. For example, while a partial DNA profile cannot prove guilt, or even contribute to doing so, it can prove innocence if interpreted correctly. "If you've got even a partial profile which contains alleles that are not present in your suspect, it isn't from the suspect", Barclay

2. Barbara Mayo's murderer has never been brought to justice, although Derbyshire Police have identified a viable suspect whom they believe is the killer, but he has not been charged and is unlikely ever to face trial for medical reasons.

explained. "It doesn't just suggest that—it means they did not do it in that particular case. You'd have to, as we know the Americans do, invent all sorts of reasons why the person who they said raped and killed this woman is then, 'Okay the DNA inside her doesn't match means he was just standing by watching or holding her hand or something'. It is just bollocks. They don't want to admit they made mistakes".

There are practical examples of this attitude and it is not confined to the USA—the Schiedammer Park crimes that Richard Eikelenboom has explained previously is a classic example of inconvenient partial profiles requiring an explanation, however unlikely that turned out to be. That didn't happen in the USA. It has happened in Britain too, in a notorious case with striking similarities to the belatedly resolved Schiedammer Park crimes. There are others too and general lessons to be learned in such circumstances. But this should never happen because the integrity of the forensic scientist should prevent it. The science should speak for itself in such cases—there should be no dispute, but sadly the wrong mentality sometimes prevails, especially if an expert thinks that their job is to support the case that the team that instructed them wants.

"My job is to produce the evidence that they've got the wrong person", Barclay said. "I could care less about the position of the courts because in the last few years when I started working for the defence, I've been a bit horrified about the hoops that some jurisdictions will go through to avoid making it obvious that they've made a mistake and I've got no power to rectify that. All I can do is provide my evidence for the defence or the prosecution and I was a bit naïve until relatively recently, because I believed not only that the system was quite good, which inevitably means that some guilty people get off, but I also believed that if evidence can be put forward that somebody hadn't done it that something would be done about it".

Sadly, that is not always the case, but the integrated approach championed by Barclay is undoubtedly an important tool that can prevent the opportunity for justice to miscarry. It can also result in putting investigations back on the right track whether a miscarriage of justice had occurred previously or not.

CHAPTER 45

The Safety Nets

Review

While it was plainly necessary to integrate forensic pathology into the requirements of modern police investigations, would review by colleagues at the same practice work?[1] After all, self-regulation has a long and wretched history of failure everywhere it has been tried, which included the Lynette White Inquiry more than once. None of the inquiries since the collapse of the Police Corruption Trial have addressed this glaring failing. Theresa May's solution is to gaze into the entrails of the one aspect of the case that has been reviewed more than once — the very same thing that emphasises the failure of this approach. South Wales Police — good intentions notwithstanding — should not have been allowed anywhere near Phase III. They wanted to put right what they had got wrong, but even with the best will they faced forces that wanted sleeping dogs to lie and still do.

A decision was taken to investigate and prosecute. It was a disastrous decision. The opportunity to obtain the truth by offering amnesty, if necessary, was lost. Not only did it gain nothing, but it cost plenty. The only convictions obtained — the New Cardiff Three — was another miscarriage of justice. The alleged eyewitnesses (Mark Grommek, Angela Psaila and Learnne Vilday) were forced to lie. They had told the truth for months, only to be bullied into submission and then be prosecuted and jailed for telling the lies demanded. Their treatment was deemed to be 'unacceptable in a civilised society', by Mr Justice (Sir David) Maddison. But even after the Police Corruption Trial collapsed, the

1. The Home Office established the Pathology Delivery Board after the collapse of the Lynette White Police Corruption Trial. Part of its remit is control of forensic pathologists and sanction of them if they do not meet the standard required. The circumstances that led to it being set up and its work will be discussed in greater detail in the **FIP**'s forthcoming publication, **Forensic Pathology: Righting Wrongs**.

alleged eyewitnesses remain convicted—the only people to be punished over one of Britain's most notorious miscarriages of justice.

Once the Police Corruption Trial failed ignominiously, yet more self-regulation was imposed without public scrutiny. The IPCC and HMCPSI investigations were limited in scope—deliberately. The terms of reference excluded the original investigation. Decisions on how the system that had failed miserably would be investigated were taken by the very system that had failed miserably. Dismal failure was rewarded with exclusion of the very thing that had made an investigation of what had gone wrong necessary—the original egregious miscarriage of justice. It beggars belief that time after time the reward of self-regulation is offered and failure is rewarded at public expense.

Exceptions?

Nevertheless, Professor Barclay thinks that it could work in forensic pathology. He points out that even though the reviews are carried out within the group of three, there are other safeguards too. As he mentioned previously: "All the reports are put on a National Database, which is restricted to forensic pathologists, and they're accessible to all the other forensic pathologists, so they can be read and are read by everybody, but only by a forensic pathologist".

Even though forensic pathologists can now access the reports of colleagues—and raise concerns if they have them—the original review was conducted by direct colleagues. If this system had been in place before the recent scandals in forensic pathology resulted in the removal from the Home Office Register of Forensic Pathologists, of among others Paula Lannas and Michael Heath, a serious flaw would have emerged. Lannas and Heath would have reviewed each other's work. Would they have found fault with each other's work?

"I still think they might have done", Barclay said.

But he does not think that the reviewing within the group of three is the main reason it would work. "Even so, putting people in a group of three, that's very difficult to say that it must be effective on its own. It can't be just that group of three, but people can look at the reports and as far as I know many of the complaints about the pathologists you mention, actually came from within the forensic pathology system. There was no difficulty in finding other pathologists to say that they weren't performing well".

It is absolutely correct to say that the downfall of both Heath and Lannas was precipitated by forensic pathologists who were concerned about the poor standard of their work and reported it. So Barclay thinks that it would and does work, and he has a point. It plainly did in reference to both Heath and Lannas and also Peter Acland and Freddy Patel.

"You have to justify your actions, but it's saying to them up front, and it does say to them up front, 'You are part of the investigative team, the same as a forensic scientist'", he said. "There is no primacy and in the past many pathologists felt they had primacy and I've seen some super examples of that".

Investigative Opportunities

The issue of primacy that many pathologists felt entitled to was one that Barclay had mentioned previously. Along with Burdiss and Pugh, Barclay ensured that procedures were developed to tackle it, because it was essential to appreciate the different opportunities to obtain physical evidence. It was also vital to appreciate how that could be compromised through competition and practices that sacrificed the importance of some evidence compared to other techniques and sciences.

Barclay explains the process. "Supposing you're stabbed and I'm looking for fibres and hairs to link you to the offender — the contact points — because it's a close contact crime", Barclay said. "If I allow the pathologist to have primacy and he wants to turn the body over to take anal swabs or something like that or he wants the body removed because it's in a dangerous place and he wants the body taken away in a body bag, well, that loses that fibre and hair evidence because when I said you've been stabbed, you're leaking. You leak all over the inside of the body bag and that removes the fibres from where they were originally, so it's got to be the SIO who decides, 'No in this case, we won't let the pathologist touch it until it gets back to the mortuary'. I think that's a big change and it's quite a sensible change too and in the UK as a matter of routine, we would tape the body at the scene and that it would be a forensic scientist that would do that".

These changes protect the integrity of the evidence, but the course of the investigations will reflect the views of the SIO and the interests of the police. So what about the needs of defendants? Barclay thinks that the availability of defence pathologists is an important counter-balance to protect their needs. "Well anybody with an interest can challenge anybody else's opinion anyway", he said. "I don't see that as being odd and I'm sure it happened in the past as well. Now it's quite easy to find a pathologist who would have a look at a case. There always was a system in the UK where you had a defence pathologist who wasn't supposedly related to the original pathologist acting on behalf of a defendant even if you haven't solved the crime, but it should be easier now as a matter of routine for someone to find a second pathology opinion, but people will always complain about inquests and so on".

But is it that simple?[2]

Victims' Rights

While some cases—perhaps many—will have no merit and do not deserve review, the baby should not be cast out with the bathwater. It is well known that pathologists have made errors in the past—some of these errors were very serious and led to miscarriages of justice. Some deaths that should have been classed as homicides have not been and others that should not have been were. So what should be done about that? Both the families of 'potential victims' and those protesting innocence have options, but are those enough? Barclay thinks they are, because the defendant has the right to have a second post-mortem examination conducted for the defence, even if the offender has not been identified yet and those alleging homicide after an initial post-mortem examination

2. It was not always a simple matter obtaining access to quality forensic pathology services for defendants. In a forthcoming **FIP** publication **Forensic Pathology: Next Time The Fire** a case mangled by forensic pathology and the primacy of the forensic pathologist will demonstrate in detail these dangers, and the lack of means to correct errors caused by an 'expert' who was later removed from the Home Office Register of Forensic Pathologists. Astonishingly, Charles Miskin, the QC, who relied on that expert's opinion against Neil Sayers, later led the case against Michael Heath at the tribunal that ended his career as a Home Office pathologist. This contradiction and the effects of Heath's opinions in that case has never been redressed.

have reached a different conclusion or were inconclusive, can have it reviewed or get another post-mortem examination conducted.

"But they (relatives) do have the same rights", he said, "but they would have to pay for a second post-mortem and so on, or get somebody to do it pro bono".

He does not think that a second post-mortem should be automatically conducted at public expense, even when the post-mortem result shows a non-malicious death. For him, anyone wanting to challenge the original opinion should have to pay for the privilege. "They absolutely should [have to pay themselves], because every person, who's lost somebody, maybe 25% of them, get ludicrously upset about it", he said before clarifying what he meant. "It's got to be somebody's fault and so on and I think you'd have it again and again and again. You'd have every case going through the courts".

So Barclay does not believe that every case needs a second post-mortem or review after review and he's right, but nevertheless there are other cases — worthy ones that have slipped through cracks previously. What will stop that happening again in the future? "There is no system in place that would second guess whether somebody has made a mistake in any individual case, but the fail-safe is that you always can get somebody to do a review of it", he said. "You might have to pay them admittedly. There is no automatic right of review in every case and I don't think it would be possible to do that".

Perhaps not, but justice should not depend on wealth. There has to be a better and fairer way that dispenses justice on the merit of the case, rather than the ability to pay for a review. After all, there have been cases that have never been reviewed despite controversy, even when the pathologist has been removed from the Home Office Register of Forensic Pathologists.

CHAPTER 46

Demoralisation

The Effects of Closure

In 2012 the government shut down the Forensic Science Service. Despite its failures, and there were high profile ones, the FSS was viewed with respect in forensic science circles and rightly so. It not only provided expert analysis and testimony, but conducted research that resulted in the next generation of forensic science testing. That avenue of much needed research has closed for ever. It has also led to talented forensic scientists becoming demoralised and leaving the profession, causing a shortage of qualified experts. Forensic science and relevant expertise on the cheap is no solution. Nevertheless, Rennison does not think that the impact of closure is as significant as many thought it would be.

"The impact on quality is negligible and there's good evidence to prove this", Rennison said. "Right at the very beginning I wrote to Ministers about this, and Ministers supporting this said, 'Whatever work is taken out of the FSS and allocated elsewhere, it's got to go to people with the right quality management systems', so it's taken out of the FSS who had the quality management systems and it can only go to organisations with similar quality management systems, so there's a lot of effort put in to the measuring of the quality management systems of the other organisations. I spent a lot of time on this with colleagues from the National Police Improvement Agency".[1]

That helped to limit the damage in terms of maintaining quality. "I mean they were able to ensure that work was only allocated to groups that could maintain the quality", Rennison said. "It took a huge effort and it did cause some disruptions in terms of the backlog of turnaround times, but those are now being managed out of the system because don't

1. The NPIA was itself shut down in October 2013. All operations were transferred to the National College of Policing (NCP) and the Serious Organised Crime Agency (SOCA) by December 2012. SOCA was itself replaced by the National Crime Agency (NCA) the following year.

forget the FSS did have 65% of the market, but there was also at the same time a huge downturn in police demand. They started pushing far less cases through to save money quite frankly, so the net result was all the work that was allocated was reallocated to businesses which saw their businesses grow rapidly. They made very clear and correct efforts to assess their ability to grow and maintain quality and they all passed the test, so quality has been maintained, but there have been impacts in other directions".

Causes for Concern

One of the biggest causes for concern is the loss of talent from forensic sciences that occurred with the closure of the FSS. "Staff leaving the business, so the FSS has seen a lot of its people who were not taken on by other companies, so just left", Rennison said. "Some of them set up small consultancies. Others just left the forensic science world very disillusioned, which is sad, but that happens when things downsize hugely and rapidly. There is a huge reduction in capacity, but matched by an equal reduction in police demand. There's been a slight disruption in turnaround times. There's been a lot of staff reorganisation going on, but thankfully quality has been kept on an even keel".

Nevertheless, forensic science, at every level has lost people from the profession who could still have contributed and an area that is still in desperate need is chronically understaffed and under-resourced. The effect on the quality of forensic sciences is obvious. It is ironic that this is occurring at a time when it has been difficult to keep pace with advances in forensic science. A few decades ago under-estimating the importance of these sciences and investigative policing had dire consequences. The errors made during the investigation of the crimes committed by the Yorkshire Ripper eventually resulted in the National Crime Faculty being established in 1996 to ensure that investigative opportunities were not missed. Later known as National Crimes and Operations Faculty, and by various other names such as the National Centre for Policing Excellence (NCPE) and the National Policing Improvement Agency, it helped to pioneer the integrated approach to investigations, with experienced detectives, forensic scientists, and psychologists being attached to major enquiries right from the start. But there is a gap in the process—a big one. There is no similar resource for defendants. "It's essential that they get better organised", Rennison said. "There's a huge issue around defence access to experts. I think there is a growing concern. The President of the Supreme Court, Neuberger[2] commented on this. His concern's around the reduction in legal aid spending on these issues. I think those are presenting bigger risks to our criminal justice system in the future than the closing of the FSS—the downturn in capacity".

It is certainly a worry, made even worse by the current government's determination to achieve swingeing cuts in legal aid. Access to forensic science for defendants is seen as a low priority. It is such short-sighted thinking that allowed the truth of the Lynette White Inquiry, among many others, to remain concealed for so long and for the cost to mount without achieving understanding of what had happened and what lessons could be learned. Rather than achieve fiscal responsibility, these policies wasted a fortune without delivering justice or accountability.

2. Baron (David) Neuberger was appointed the second President of the Supreme Court of the United Kingdom on October 1st 2012, succeeding Baron (Nicholas) Phillips of Worth Maltravers. In October 2017 Baroness (Brenda) Hale of Richmond replaced Neuberger. The comments that Rennison refers to were made by Neuberger a couple of days before my interview with the then FSR.

CHAPTER 47

Fresh Start

Lessons Learned

Professor Barclay explains the particular advantages of the integrated approach to cold cases in greater detail. "I think the essential thing is that you start fresh, as if the crime had just happened, but you've already got the benefit of lots of documentation and so on to go through, so I guess the first thing to do is to retrieve all that documentation and all the physical items that you can", he said. "Some physical items will be stored at the laboratories and some physical items like clothing and stuff like that will be stored hopefully in the actual police stores. The difficulty was in the old days and probably will be again now the FSS [Forensic Science Service] has gone, that stuff is scattered all over the place".

The closure of the FSS posed serious problems detailed in previous chapters. This adds to the mess. "In some cases we can recover all the original physical items like the clothing, knickers and so on and we can analyse those afresh", Barclay said. "In other cases we don't get any of that back from the police because they've had them destroyed and we have to go for what we would call recovered items in the laboratory — that's things like microscope slides, tapings and things like that. Often the Forensic Science Service was the only source of that sort of material. They had a giant store somewhere in Birmingham, which they kept not only items which they'd created like microscope slides and stuff like that, but also the by-products of DNA testing, just swabs that had been extracted. Now we can extract them again, so that's recovery of the actual physical stuff. Then we need to set that in context and we'll be looking particularly when we're doing a reinvestigation for things that just don't make sense".

The abolition of the FSS has potentially cost many inquiries access to material like this. The archive of FSS material may or may not have stored this material and preserved access to it. That material could be vital in several cases, as Barclay explains.

"What is the reason why we *haven't* got something and a realisation that the absence of a piece of evidence that *should* be there may be as significant as the presence of something?" he asks. "It's true that the lack of evidence—the absence of a particular bit of evidence—is not evidence that a person is not there because we might not have found it, but if it's been looked for and it's not there, then it probably means something else happened, something we haven't identified and so that would be what I would call an anomaly—something that doesn't quite make sense. You can't explain everything that happened in every murder or rape, but if you got a significant anomaly—something that really doesn't make sense, then you should really look for an explanation, because it may mean that the whole context—the whole sequence of events is different" [his emphasis].

And this is another reason why the FSS archive must be preserved and accessed whenever necessary—not only for material that may still be testable, but for original records, notes and statements. There will in the future be cases that require cold case review years after a conviction is quashed. Should they be left in limbo unable to be vindicated because records cannot be located? It doesn't matter how good a test is if there is nothing to test, or it simply cannot be found. This is yet another disastrous consequence of the abolition of the FSS.

Anomalies

In virtually all investigations there will not be a shortage of things that don't make sense. Obviously the significant ones could make the difference between resolution and justice and the failure to resolve the case. However, not all anomalies are significant. Barclay explains the difference. "Well a minor inconvenience might be something for which there isn't an explanation, but it doesn't alter the way you perceive the sequence of events at the crime", Barclay says. "The sequence of events is you should be able to work out exactly where the encounter was, where the attack-site was, where the dump-site was, if it is a dump-site and so on. An example of something that is more important than that is you've got a body which is alleged to be left at the attack-site; and on her legs are some parallel scratches and when you look at the crime-scene — admittedly this a cold case, so we're looking at it some months afterwards — we can't see anything that could have produced those scratches on the knees and that's something that is obviously very significant, because how did those happen?"

As Barclay had clearly demonstrated, the scratches were a very significant anomaly in that case.

"They would have been painful", Barclay said before explaining why the scratches were vitally important information. "It's not something that happened accidentally and it indicates that that person has not been attacked at the site where her body was found, because there's nothing there that could have produced those scratches. She was attacked somewhere else and in that case we had a big job to persuade the police that that wasn't an attack-site — that it was actually a dump-site. And the reason for that was it *had* to be an attack-site [for the police] because the main suspect — the person who had been arrested — was her boyfriend who didn't drive and had no access to a vehicle, so if it's actually a dump-site, then she's been killed somewhere else and she's been driven there and the body's been dumped. And it's not him. So eventually we found out that those scratches on the inside of her left thigh and knee came from her being dragged over the bar of a pick-up truck, which had been coated with anti-slip paint. And, so yes, it was true, she was attacked somewhere else — she had been transported in that pick-up truck and then the body had been dumped. So, that's a significant anomaly — something that couldn't possibly have happened at the crime-scene if the scenario of the police was correct" [his emphasis].

CHAPTER 48

All in Play

Effects

Despite his competence and those of his successors, Spilsbury and Spilsburyism adversely affected the criminal justice system long after Sir Bernard took his own life. Spilsbury had been given a status that towered above others in his profession and allowed pathologists to influence the course of investigations at the expense of other forensic sciences, as Spilsbury's pre-eminence in investigations was bequeathed to his profession. The changes in forensic pathology that Mick Burdiss, Gary Pugh and Professor Barclay helped to incorporate are therefore very welcome, but pre-eminence of forensic pathology was far from the only issue that had to be tackled. Barclay and others showed that the dangers sometimes extended far beyond pre-eminence and into a mind-set where a few pathologists saw themselves as aloof from and even above police investigators. That had to change and it did, but there were other problems too—huge ones.

Pathology affected other forensic sciences too. There will be cases where defence lawyers don't understand that and the experts that they instructed do not realise it either. For example, forensic entomology. What happens when maggots are discovered in or near a body and a forensic entomologist has not been called to the scene, or is not available? Who collects the maggots and relevant data? How is that done? How is it stored? What happens to the maggots afterwards? In at least one case that we know about, the pathologist made a pig's ear of it. Suffice to say the pathologist—later disgraced—failed to ensure that the evidence the maggots could have provided was obtained.[1] This is yet another example of the dangers of primacy. That pathologist's knowledge of forensic entomology

1. This is the case of Neil Sayers. The forensic pathologist, Michael Heath, got it badly wrong and there were dire consequences, which over 20 years later, have not been corrected. For further details see **FIP**'s forthcoming book **Forensic Pathology: Next Time The Fire**.

was not good enough — important evidence was lost as a result. That is unacceptable. Imagine a blood stained handkerchief being thrown away without being tested. Couldn't happen? It happened to maggots in a case where they represented the only realistic opportunity to establish when a significant event in the horrible crime took place. Without primacy of forensic pathologists — undeserved on any view in this case — would that mess have occurred?

"And that's a classic example of where much more research is needed", Rennison said. "You're into a very, very niche area of knowledge. Entomology and fires and the extent of it is hugely complex and hugely variable from circumstance to circumstance, so you're going to be if something can exist in that area it will vary its behaviour very differently day to day, hour to hour. So it's under the circumstances, which is why I think replicating experiments become very, very demanding, because you can't replicate all the variables, where they don't exist in every set of circumstances. I think under those sort of circumstances these mistakes could happen again, which is why my work with entomologists is to publish guidance on standards on this issue. One of the biggest problems with sciences such as entomology is that if you read the Police Murder and Investigation Manual, there was a section in it where the first time the forensic entomologist appears or is talked about is in the post-mortem".

The problem with this should be obvious. Forensic entomology is relevant far earlier than during the post-mortem. It also presupposes that access to that Manual is commonplace. It is not, but should be, as that is how investigative methods and conduct can be evaluated. This is especially important in complex cases. It requires sampling from different areas of the remains, establishing environmental conditions and much more as there are many factors that affect the rate of development of the maggots, such as body temperature and ambient temperature and much more besides. Each area sampled requires a fixed sample too — that establishes the stage of development at a given time and conditions. Police should also be advised on how to rear the maggots if a forensic entomologist is not available to do so. All of this should have been done before the post-mortem examination.

Other Sciences

There is a perception in members of the public that any case should have DNA evidence. It doesn't always happen. Absence of evidence is not, on its own, evidence of absence. As occurred with the maggots referred to above, a lack of awareness can cause evidence to be lost as well. Richard Eikelenboom explained the difficulties in the Schiedammer case regarding the transportation of evidence along with an asphyxiated body. But there is far more than DNA that needs to be integrated into investigations. "They're all included", Rennison said. "We manage the quality standards around forensic pathology. I have a specialist group chaired by Professor Harry Millward-Sadler that advises on that. Dr Jeff Adams leads on that for me. We're about to publish a whole new raft of guidelines on forensic pathology and for the first time ever standards for forensic mortuaries; it's never happened up until now, so that's been included. Entomology, yes. I meet with entomologists. The Codes of Practice and Conduct I've published is the standard for everyone, so all forensic sciences have to go through generic procedures such as collection, continuity, proper storage of and handling of exhibits, etc."

Establishing standards was a gradual process. The case that I referred to above happened two decades ago. Part of the reason the entomological evidence was mangled was because of the legacy of primacy that forensic pathologists — even unworthy ones — enjoyed.

"We are now picking up the knowledge required to build the standards required for specific disciplines, so we're about to publish a new standard for forensic archaeology and we worked hand in glove with the Institute of Archaeology to do that", Rennison said. "We've worked hand in glove with a new organisation, representing UK toxicologists to set a new set of standards for UK toxicology. We've had meetings with the forensic anthropologists. If you add up all the different disciplines — there's about 60 or 70 of them — so entomology, fingerprints, shoe-marks and so on. Over the next three years all of those have to set standards and guidance built to hang on the back of my generic framework — entomology, you name it, they're all in play".

But the fiscal constraints and abolition of the FSS have thrown a huge spanner in the works — one that could lead to further injustices.

CHAPTER 49

Hypotheses

Disastrous

The Forensic Science Service had been strongly criticised over their performance in several cases and, in my opinion, that contributed to the end of the FSS. The loss of confidence that these injustices caused and the rise of market forces contributed to its demise. While Rennison sees some positives, Barclay does not. It drove down prices, but it also demoralised forensic scientists as was detailed previously. Babies and bathwater spring to mind.

"I think it's a very bad thing because we had a unique advantage which people worldwide thought the UK had", Barclay said. "We had one major police force organisation ACPO [the Association of Chief Police Officers—ACPOS in Scotland] and we had one major service provider, the FSS, so if somebody wanted to introduce a new method of packaging or a new technique or a new way of handling things at crime-scenes, they could do it together instantly. That would be impossible in the United States. Now the FSS has gone there are dozens of small forensic providers and there will be many police forces that set up their own labs. The standard of quality assurance is likely to be very, very variable to put it politely and it's impossible to do things nationally in the way it was before".

There will be the accreditation processes and quality controls that Rennison mentioned previously, but safeguards are only as effective as the zeal with which they are enforced, and also the consequences for breaking them. However, despite the accreditation standards, the Damilola Taylor Inquiry was derailed by serious error in the forensic science. Sian Hedges missed clearly visible bloodstains on one of Danny Preddie's trainers. Along with his brother Ricky, the Preddie brothers were the main suspects. Had this and other staining on their clothing been noticed when Hedges did her work, the 2002 trial may have been avoided and they would have been brought to justice far earlier. Hedges' error was discovered belatedly and tests proved that it was indeed Damilola's blood. The Preddie brothers were convicted of manslaughter and an inquiry headed by Brian Caddy reviewed the failings made by the FSS—Hedges really. Among its tasks was making recommendations to both the Home Secretary and board of the FSS on whether changes were required to its examination procedures, recruitment, training and management of forensic scientists by the FSS. Finally, Caddy's review had the power to make whatever recommendations it deemed necessary on the future role of the Forensic Regulator in overseeing applicable standards to all suppliers of forensic services to the criminal justice system within the UK.

The laboratory concerned had once been a Police Laboratory, but at the relevant time, it was run by the FSS. The error did not surface in peer-review, because it could only have done so if the relevant photos that clearly showed the blood staining had been provided to the peer-reviewer. That would not have happened, as these suspects had been wrongly eliminated previously due to the error and consequently, none of this information was in the statement to be peer-reviewed. The error that occurred in this case may have surfaced earlier if a fresh pair of eyes had been allowed to review Hedges' work at the time. In fact, it clearly would have done, as that is precisely what happened in the cold case review that led to the correct resolution of Damilola Taylor's death. As we have seen already, peer-reviewing is a long-established safeguard designed to catch errors. But it made no difference in the Lynette White Inquiry and could not have caught the error in the Damilola Taylor Inquiry too. There is no record that Whiteside's work in the Lynette White Inquiry was peer-reviewed as was required. And what of the records? The delay in investigating this fully has caused problems as it is unclear if the original records still exist in the FSS archive. If safeguards are to be effective, there has to be consequences for failing to adhere to them. In this case, there were not. But there are other causes for concern.

Police Labs and Standards

Laboratories run by the police are no solution. The pressures for forensic scientists to see themselves as working for the police in such situations are obvious whether overt or just perceived. An obvious example of the dangers of this approach is Oklahoma's experience. Joyce Gilchrist was once the darling of law enforcement, but her fall from grace illustrated the serious flaws in both her work and a criminal justice system that tolerated and relied on her. She was involved in several undoubted miscarriages of justice. "Gilchrist is the sort of person who you might have a bit like Dr Clift — people who make a mistake or shortcut or are too involved with the police or whatever and that can happen anywhere", Barclay says. "It's just easier to sort those people out if everybody in the organisation is adhering to one system, so that anybody who isn't stands out more, as Dr Clift did. It was his colleagues in the FSS at Birmingham who uncovered his failings".

Despite concerns being raised over Gilchrist previously, she continued to offer fibre and hair matching evidence that went far beyond the limits of the science and that resulted in convictions that should never have been obtained. Jeffrey Pierce was an innocent man. It took far too long — the best part of fifteen years — to vindicate him. DNA eventually proved him innocent. It proved that Gilchrist had wronged him terribly and the delays in proving his innocence resulted in another injustice. The statute of limitations ran out. Despite knowing that Omer May Jnr was the real perpetrator there was nothing that could be done. The refusal to acknowledge Pierce's innocence for so long had ensured that a vicious rapist evaded sanction for his crime. So how can it be prevented?

"You initially start any investigation by trying to work out what happened", Barclay said. "As I mentioned before, in physical evidence, we're after contact points. We can use those contact points as soon as we know if our hypothesis is right. There must have been contact at these points. We should have found results and you can use those actual physical findings to prove or disprove that hypothesis. When you start, you often have four or five different hypotheses — we don't care. What we're going to do is disprove them until we're left with the thing that actually happened. In the case of Lynette White, the original hypothesis was that it was a single male that had done it and cast-off blood at the scene. Everything that was ever found agreed with that. Nothing that was ever found, including the blood grouping that matched Angela Psaila, disagreed with that initial hypothesis. So, one of the questions that you have to ask is why was that abandoned in court? There wasn't a good reason for it to be abandoned".

CHAPTER 50

Integration and Competence

Integration

The Lynette White Inquiry is a classic example of the need for an integrated approach to the crime-scene evidence and forensic science. If that had happened, a very clear picture would never have become distorted. The importance of the integrated approach cannot be emphasised too highly. The importance of fibres and, even more so, DNA have been highlighted, but there are other forensic sciences that have been affected by pathology-related issues. Forensic entomology is a science that can offer useful evidence, enabling investigators to establish the post-mortem interval. It too cannot tell you precisely when a murder occurred, but it can give investigators a range to work with. However, forensic entomologists are not always available at the drop of a hat. Consequently, they may have to depend on others to establish the environmental information that they require. In such circumstances they also require others to obtain entomological samples and to treat them in the manner recommended by forensic entomologists. In the case mentioned earlier in this section, that did not happen. The consequences of this failure were dire.

It illustrates the fact that competent forensic pathologists have to be fully conversant with such requirements and in the absence of a forensic entomologist, they have to be prepared to ensure that the integrity and quality of the entomological evidence is guaranteed so the forensic entomologist gets the best opportunity to establish the optimum evidence that the entomological samples can give. Forensic entomology is capable of establishing a likely range of times within which a significant post-mortem event, such as burning or partially burning a body, or even death, took place. However, the quality of evidence obtained will depend on the efficiency, competence and even integrity of the forensic pathologist who took those samples and the advice given to investigators regarding how those samples should be treated if a forensic entomologist was not available to collect and rear the maggots. In short, it is clear why the integrated approach championed by Barclay and Burdiss and Pugh was necessary and why forensic pathology had to be integrated into the requirements of the SIOs, kicking and screaming if necessary. A decade after the Lynette White Inquiry fiasco, the entomological disaster showed how little had been learned. The integrated approach had yet to be enforced.

Competence

Like any science, forensic pathology depends upon the efficiency, competence and integrity of the practitioner. It would be churlish in the extreme not to acknowledge that the vast majority of forensic pathologists performed and perform their duties with due diligence and expertise. Some inevitably fall below their usual high standards on rare occasions. There is nothing sinister in that. However, there are others whose work is simply not up to standard. Over the years forensic sciences have developed. Currently, new techniques and methods are being discovered and utilised at a rapid rate, but this brings new challenges.

The evidence must be allowed to speak honestly. Hypotheses must be properly tested and tested again, so errors can be caught and corrected and rapidly. Peer-review is an obvious method to achieve that, yet safeguards are only as efficient as the zeal with which they are observed and the consequences for breaching them must be sufficient to ensure compliance. John Whiteside is not a forensic pathologist, but his conduct, and indeed that of his employers, offers a stark warning. Either Whiteside evaded peer-review in one case, and did so in circumstances that suggest it was deliberate, or for some unknown reason the established procedures just happened to break down in this of all cases. Whiteside knew why his work should be peer-reviewed and that it was standard practice for it to occur. His final hypothesis in the Lynette White Inquiry was extremely controversial, to it put mildly. It defied logic and the evidence too. It was precisely the type of thing that peer-review was designed to test robustly. Although meetings occurred where Peter Gill, Trevor Howitt and Nicholas Prance raised concerns, this was not peer-review. Whiteside's statements should have been rigorously examined and his conclusions tested, by asking him to explain the basis of his opinions. This is exactly what peer-review was for.

The usual evidence of peer-review was absent. There is no reason for that to have happened. It should have been counter-signed. It wasn't. If it was peer-reviewed then the peer-reviewer has nailed his own reputation to Whiteside's hypothesis too, meaning that the subsequent demolition of its credibility should affect the peer-reviewer too. There is no evidence that Whiteside's various hypotheses to explain away the anomalies, had ever happened before or since and the evidence does not support it here either. The delay in addressing this failure has prevented resolution of it. Memories have faded. Whiteside and his colleagues cannot remember if it was peer-reviewed, or even who should have done it, and with the abolition of the FSS any records will be difficult to locate unless they are in the archive. Whoever was responsible for peer-reviewing Whiteside must account for the apparent failing. The FSS does not emerge with credit from this either. It had safeguards and procedures, which it seems to have failed to enforce and worse still, there were no consequences for any of these failings. Hopefully forensic pathology will learn from this and ensure that such safeguards are efficient and effective in the present and future too.

Conclusion

Spilsburyed — Eminence and Integration

As we have seen, the history of forensic pathology offers many lessons, and not just for that particular forensic science. Professor Sir Bernard Spilsbury's pre-eminent status in the field was dangerous for many reasons. It resulted in a collision course between the science and the needs of an integrated approach to modern investigative policing. The clash was inevitable and in fact, necessary. It could and should have occurred decades earlier and were it not for Spilsbury's aura and authority, sometimes in the face of the evidence, it probably would have done. The cult of Spilsbury was dangerous, but important, and in part the price that forensic pathology had to pay to evolve from its tag of the 'beastly profession'. Spilsbury and his mentor established the credibility of the discipline, but their practices also set the use of forensic pathology in the courts back many decades, as it stood above the needs of investigations and ultimately resulted in mistakes that led to injustices. Spilsbury may have brought forensic pathology from out of obscurity and into acceptance, but the price was high — too high. It set the tone for future investigations — the dominance of forensic pathology over other forensic sciences throughout most of the 20th century, and indeed into the 21st too. That should never have happened. It contributed to investigations going awry.

The roots of the problem stem from Spilsbury and Spilsburyism. Judges, juries and even some of his peers frequently acquiesced to him — the force of his personality and reputation could and did trump evidence on occasion. 'It's Spilsbury. He must be right', was not an uncommon opinion, but it came with great danger, as it shaped the conduct of investigations and even trials. This is still a basic defect of our adversarial system — whoever has the firmest opinions will always be most popular with the CPS, the prosecution and the legal profession. Lawyers always want black and white answers, even when truth is obviously best expressed in shades of grey. This suggests that the integrated approach needs to be expanded beyond the investigative process and into the judicial too. There were, however, some pathologists who dared to oppose Spilsbury in his prime, such as Sir Sydney Smith and Robert Brontë. But Spilsbury was Spilsbury — arrogant and dominating the theatre of the court. The cold comfort for Smith and Brontë when the verdict went against them of probably being right made little difference — the injustices had still occurred and every time they did, Spilsbury's standing and opinions in the profession were strengthened. Even on his rare forays into defence work, Spilsbury could not countenance being wrong. On two occasions it appears certain that he was wrong and that there were dire consequences in both cases — murderers went free as a result. Rarely Spilsbury went too far, even for the public. That tended to occur in cases that offended his conservative views. He was even prepared to allow a soldier to hang because he disapproved of homosexuality and allowed his opposition to abortion to colour evidence against a doctor — a prosecution that should never have been brought — in a case where a child had been raped and became pregnant as a result. Even in the great pathologist's lifetime that was too much, and Spilsbury's reputation took a deserved hit.

Effect, Consequences and Progress

But Spilsbury was the first superstar pathologist. No expert other than Spilsbury could have had such an effect on his profession, investigative methods and the public from which jurors are drawn, at that time, but as his powers waned, the dangers of Spilsburyism and indeed the man himself became more pronounced. His opinions trumped justice and even evidence. No expert — however experienced or gifted — should be allowed to dominate her/his profession, especially when he occasionally allowed that dominance to reflect his political views rather than allow the evidence to lead him wherever it will. Spilsbury offers graphic testimony to the dangers of anyone holding so much sway over such a profession where the consequences of error could and did cost lives, but there was a bigger problem — one that outlived the 'Father of Forensics'. Eminence, or even pre-eminence, survived Spilsbury, but even the next generation had their notable failures, despite lacking his status. Donald Teare and

Keith Simpson were undoubtedly at the top of their profession, but made very serious errors, even though their mistakes paled in comparison to that of Professor James Cameron in the Maxwell Confait Inquiry. Teare, Simpson and Francis Camps were the top forensic pathologists of the post-Spilsbury era. But the basic problem remained.

All of these errors occurred in the era of the 'ultimate peer-review' — trial — as the defining method of holding forensic pathologists accountable for their conclusions and practices. But that indicated another problem. The work of forensic pathologists was not peer-reviewed, even in the modern era, and that meant that errors or bad practices were not caught in time. Too often the trial process failed to halt or correct miscarriages of justice in the making and appeals were hit and miss. But perhaps a greater flaw was in respect of homicides that were wrongly ruled to be natural causes. Obviously, there would be no trial process in such cases and consequently, it could not have the 'ultimate peer-review' to correct the error. Cold case reviews could achieve that and did in some cases, but in others the damage had already been done.

The Police and Criminal Evidence Act (PACE) became law and the Crown Prosecution Service was established in the 1980s. The Police Complaints Board (PCB) and its successor, the Police Complaints Authority (PCA), came and went, but despite progress in the Forensic Science Service on peer-review, there were loop-holes and pathologists stayed aloof from the safeguards for decades. It took almost a century after Spilsbury's emergence to integrate forensic pathologists into the modern investigative process. That required forensic pathologists to understand that decisions had to be taken by the SIO, who was ultimately responsible, and that they (the pathologists) were part of a team and definitely not the gaffer.

The change finally came around 2004. Gary Pugh, Mick Burdiss and Dave Barclay, on behalf of the Home Office, initiated the process that finally brought forensic pathologists into line with the requirements of modern investigations. The SIO was in charge and made decisions that the forensic pathologists had to adapt to, like it or not, and many didn't like it at all. Some left the profession over it. Previously, there were competing interests and the forensic pathologists made decisions that really ought to have been the domain of the SIO.

This change coincided with peer-review becoming a requirement. It didn't right previous wrongs, as it didn't consider them, but it provided the framework to prevent future wrongs. As such, it has to be recognised that although this was a step in the right direction, it has not and cannot right the wrongs of the past—that will require reviews and probably a new body with the tools and will to deliver. That in turn will help muster the political will to make it happen, even though the alternative is the false comfort of maintaining unjust convictions at the expense of justice, the cost of which will have to be borne by the public. Fiscal irresponsibility and wrecked lives is too high a price to pay—and keep on paying.

Safeguards

There were several safeguards that should have made a difference, but preventable injustices still occurred and were tolerated. Bizarrely, this was thought necessary (as the case of Timothy Evans illustrates) to maintain public confidence in the integrity of the criminal justice system. Ultimately, it failed and changes were made, but without deeming it necessary to redress the wrongs that had occurred. This added to the damage done to all of the victims and emphasised the fiscal irresponsibility of the ostrich-like refusal to see the problem and tackle it. There was no reason for the failure to make peer-review compulsory in forensic pathology, as it had been for years in other forensic sciences. Errors could have been prevented. And a decade or so before peer-review and integration with other forensic sciences brought forensic pathology into the era of modern investigations, accreditation requirements such as ISO 17025 ensured that quality management systems and individual competence were up to standard.

This applied in the mid-1990s, yet preventable errors continued—relevant expertise was ignored and pertinent evidence was denied its opportunity to speak. On occasion it was not even sought because the forensic pathologist deemed it unnecessary, or it was handled so poorly that the evidence was lost or compromised to the point of justice being denied. There were safeguards—at least in recent times that could and should make a difference. These safeguards were, however, only capable of being effective if they were enforced with zeal. Similarly, there had to be effective consequences for breach of those safeguards—deterrent safeguards. The Lynette White Inquiry remains a cautionary tale of the price of failing to enforce the safeguards and compounding the error by failing to apply any sanction for the breach.

Few cases illustrate the need for stringent and effective safeguards better than the Lynette White Inquiry, largely because there were safeguards that should have worked, but they did not—including peer-review, which is one of the methods of detecting and correcting errors. In that case, the peer-review safeguard failed to prevent Dr John Whiteside's outlandish cocktail-hypothesis from being advanced as evidence. There was much more besides. The crime-scene evidence, blood distribution evidence, pathology clearly indicated that Lynette had been the victim of a sustained and vicious sexually motivated homicide and that it had been committed by one man—later proved to be Jeffrey Gafoor—but this clear and logical interpretation of the evidence was distorted and manipulated until confusion reigned. Instead the evidence—massively inconvenient to the deeply flawed case against the Cardiff Five—was manipulated.

Ludicrous

The police's new hypothesis tried to square the circle, but it was a circle that ultimately could not be squared, apart from by people who fundamentally lacked scientific integrity. There was no credible evidence that was consistent with the new hypothesis—five men committing that excessively brutal murder, along with at least two witnesses in pitch darkness in a blood stained area of the room, and all seven got out of the room without leaving traces of themselves such as a blood stained fingerprint or footprint and without interfering with any of the trace evidence that eventually tied Gafoor to his crime.

It was known that foreign blood had been discovered and that the evidence showed that it had been shed by the murderer. If Professor Barclay's, or Angela Gallop's, integrated approach had been utilised, the clear picture would never have been distorted. The evidence would have prevented an easily avoidable injustice from occurring. Instead, the safeguards failed to function as intended. Furthermore, it took years for these failures to emerge, by which time the damage was beyond redress — not because it was not possible, but because the political will to right the wrongs, or even prevent repetition, did not and does not exist. Sadly, it still does not and responsibility for that rests with all three major political parties, which hoped that if they buried their heads in the sand for long enough the issues would disappear — they never did.

Dr Whiteside's original opinion was that Lynette had been murdered by one person acting on his own. There never was any credible evidence challenging this opinion, but Whiteside never explained why he changed his mind. The crime-scene and blood distribution pattern evidence entirely supported his original opinion. Despite that, Whiteside changed his opinion, based solely on the discovery that an alleged witness — a female — possessed the same combination of blood groups as the 'stranger' blood found at the scene. There was no credible evidence that it was as significant a discovery as Whiteside claimed it to be, as he knew well that the scientific evidence — Dr Peter Gill's test for the Y-chromosome — indicated that male material was present and that the Chepstow Laboratory had dealt with at least one man who possessed all of the blood groups contained in the foreign blood. The blood grouping tests were certainly credible and scientifically validated; it was his assessment of their significance that was faulty. However, Whiteside's change of opinion was not credible and his discovery was not as significant as he seemed to think for reasons detailed above. Simple mathematics showed that. 1:7600 men possessed this combination of blood groups. That means 13 out of 100,000 males would have the relevant blood groups. At the time Britain had a population of around 60 million, which meant that almost 8000 males possessed that combination of blood groups in Britain. Obviously, all bar one of those men was not involved in the murder of Lynette White. At this point a simple picture became complicated. Whiteside decided that the discovery that Psaila possessed the same 'rare' combination of blood groups was so significant that she must have been there. We now know for certain — it was pretty obvious even then — that there was not a scrap of credible evidence proving that

Angela Psaila, or any other female for that matter, had donated so much as a single cell to the foreign blood that Lynette's murderer had shed in the flat. Whiteside decided that the discovery of Psaila's blood grouping results was 'one hell of a coincidence'. But why? The blood grouping results showed that there were also approximately 8000 women who possessed the same blood groups. If the 'cocktail-hypothesis' applied to Psaila, then why not any of the other women in the 8000? Based on a population of 100,000 or so around Cardiff at the time, there would have been around 26 people who had the relevant blood groups. South Wales Police's jurisdiction at the time covered about a million people. That meant that around 260 people possessed the relevant combination of blood groups. Were all of them a hell of a coincidence too?

Peer-review is an important and mandatory safeguard designed to catch errors early. In this case, it apparently did not function as intended. Whiteside faced no sanction over the absence of a documented peer-review and nor did the person who was responsible for peer-reviewing him. That negates, or at the very least, compromises the value of peer-review. Safeguards can only be effective if there is sufficient zeal to enforce them and if the safeguard is avoided, or confusion reigns, the consequences must be strong enough to deter repetition. If that had been the case, just over a quarter of a century ago a terrible miscarriage of justice could have been avoided and a long battle to put right the injustices that followed could have been avoided.

The failure to review and expose the drastic limitations of Whiteside's 'scientifically ludicrous hypothesis' contributed to miscarriages of justice. It defied scientific logic and was never challenged as vigorously as it should have been. Back in the 1980s, PACE was new legislation—it provided protections from oppressive conduct, but there was a glaring flaw. Witnesses—no matter how important or vulnerable—were excluded from these safeguards. A heavy price was paid. Stephen Miller was bullied and hectored and that was done by officers who knew that those interviews that included shameful bullying were being recorded. At both trials the alleged eye-witnesses denied that police misconduct had occurred. By 2008, they faced trial themselves. The case had turned full circle by then, as there was no credible doubt about the innocence of the Cardiff Five due to the conviction of Jeffrey Gafoor. Professor Barclay's review and the subsequent DNA testing that occurred in Phase II of the inquiry demonstrated the inadequacy of Whiteside's work even in terms of the 1980s.

Despite having been the victims of conduct that was deemed to be 'unacceptable in a civilised society', Mark Grommek, Angela Psaila and Learnne Vilday were forced into pleading guilty to perverting the course of justice — duress, even if caused by such methods, is no defence to perjury charges in this jurisdiction. Their convictions shame the criminal justice system, as they alone have paid the price. They alone stand convicted of causing one of Britain's most notorious miscarriages of justice, while those they accused of bullying them walked free after a botched trial, or never stood trial at all. The defendants in the botched police corruption trial of 2011 are protected from further proceedings by double jeopardy, but not before they were allowed to make a mockery of what the forensic science had really said.

The forensic pathology was very clear. Lynette had been subjected to a sustained and vicious sexually motivated attack that targeted her breasts — her femininity. The cast-off blood pattern also told a story, as did the crime-scene. All of this evidence told a very clear tale — one man was responsible for all of the injuries that Lynette suffered. He committed the murder entirely on his own, in one attack. While it was 'technically' possible that there was more than one attack, there was no evidence whatsoever that this had happened. Gafoor failed to take full responsibility for all of the wounds suffered by Lynette — that does not mean that he did not inflict *all* of them. In fact, the suggestion of more than one attack is absolutely absurd for reasons Professor Barclay had made clear. How was it, that according to the police officers' defence, Gafoor attacked Lynette, inflicting comparatively minor injuries on her, cut himself in the act, and shed his blood in several places, but whoever committed the second and more brutal attack according to this scenario, used an identical knife, did not deposit a single drop of their blood in the flat or leave a single blood stained fingerprint or footprint on the way out, despite the crime occurring in the pitch black of night?

They also launched a bizarre attack on the credibility of the Phase II investigation, claiming that it should have DNA tested far more samples in that investigation, while conveniently forgetting that far more samples were tested in the Phase II investigation than had been tested in the original deeply flawed investigation and that standard and good practice was to identify what should be tested in order to assist the investigation and test only those samples. If those defence lawyers thought other samples were significant, they could, of course, have had them tested themselves. They did not do that. Instead, they chose to attack the credibility of a far more thorough and ethical investigation in order to defend the credibility of an investigation that lacked both.

A decision was taken not to prosecute Whiteside and that had an effect. If he had been a defendant, as arguably he should have been, on the basis of his opinion being unsupportable on the scientific evidence, the criticism of the Phase II investigation would have been harder to justify and Whiteside's scientifically ludicrous opinions would have been exposed for what they were. It has been suggested that Whiteside should not now face prosecution. Why not? If there is sufficient evidence and there may be, why shouldn't he be prosecuted? After all, he is not protected by double jeopardy and played a crucial part in helping the police to put Psaila in the room whilst Lynette was being murdered. That was essential in overbearing Psaila's resistance and ultimately, that of the other core witnesses. Why is it an abuse of process for him to be prosecuted now, but it is not to convict three witnesses for telling lies that they were forced to tell after several months of insisting truthfully that they knew nothing of importance about Lynette's murder, especially as Whiteside's outlandish cocktail-hypothesis was essential to 'persuade' them to become vital prosecution witnesses? The fact that they remain the only people convicted of offences relating to the miscarriage of justice suffered by the Cardiff Five, despite the way that they were treated, makes the New Cardiff Three victims of yet another miscarriage of justice, in a tawdry case that should shock the conscience. However, it doesn't appear to have achieved that. After more than three decades of persistent failed processes, that is a terrible indictment of British justice.

And there is the issue of the nature of the attack itself. Back in the 1980s, the distinguished forensic pathologist, Professor Bernard Knight, said that there were 'sexual overtones' to it. Now, the same crime would be described differently, and rightly so. The post-mortem photographs told a chilling story. Sexual overtones did not begin to describe what had happened to Lynette. The overwhelming concentration of injuries were in her chest — on and around her breasts. It was obvious that this was a sexually motivated murder and this was very significant, both from a pathology and investigative point of view. It was also very significant in legal terms, as it affected or could have affected the determination of the tariff that Gafoor should have received. There was further evidence that this was a sex crime too. Gafoor wanted the services of a prostitute — it was why he approached Lynette — and took her back to the flat which was used for that purpose. It was on any view a sex crime and that should have been adequately reflected in the tariff that Gafoor received, but as with much else, it was not.[1]

Forensic Pathology Comes of Age

It had taken the best part of a century to finally bring forensic pathology up to date with the requirements of modern policing by integrating it with other forensic sciences as part of the investigative process. The SIO was in charge, as was right — it was a police investigation of the most serious of crimes after all. But for that to happen the pre-eminent status forensic pathologists had enjoyed had to be tackled. That process reached fruition in 2004 with Barclay, Burdiss and Pugh's work for ACPO. Peer-review was required as part of it. That step was welcome, but more was required.

Various reviews had taken place over decades. This included Ralph Leishman's Report **Review of Forensic Pathology Services in England and Wales** was commissioned by the Home Office and published in 2003. The ramifications of it are certainly important, and deserve greater analysis than is possible in this book. The same applies to the 1989 Wassermann Report, and also Professor Peter Hutton's Report **A Review**

1. The tariff issues will be detailed in **FIP**'s forthcoming book **Bad Form: How Tariffs Protect the Guilty and Punish the Innocent**.

of Forensic Pathology in England and Wales which was commissioned by the then Minister of State for Crime Prevention, Norman Baker, and delivered to his successor Lynne Featherstone in March 2015.

As this book has demonstrated, there were serious problems associated with forensic pathology and its role in criminal justice system and delivery of justice for many decades. Solution began to emerge this century, and the implementation of one of them peer-review has been discussed in this book, but there were other problems and also solutions that were not addressed or resolved by peer-review. The contributions mentioned above, recommendations from them and solutions will be detailed in the **FIP**'s forthcoming publication **Forensic Pathology: Righting Wrongs** the second part of a trilogy. It will also detail the role of the Pathology Delivery Board and methods of ensuring quality services, and consequences for slipping below the required standards.

A major flaw, in my opinion at least, with peer-review is that it does not deal with the needs of the defence. Defendants have most to lose, and the least control or influence when mistakes are made, yet they bear the brunt of the problems and lack of consequences when errors are made, even in extreme circumstances. In a case that will be discussed in great detail in **Forensic Pathology: Next Time The Fire**, the last of **The Fitted-In Project**'s trilogy, despite a forensic pathologist losing his status as a Home Office Forensic Pathologist, a review of CCRC cases involving that expert, there has been no review of his role in this case—a case where his performance had dire consequences. This has happened in a case where Charles Miskin QC relied on Michael Heath's expert opinion against Neil Sayers, and later was the QC who brought the case against Heath at the tribunal which resulted in him losing his status as a Home Office pathologist.

Forensic pathology, like any forensic science, has no side, and that should be reflected in its delivery by forensic pathologists. The requirements of defendants will be examined in greater detail in the second and third parts of this trilogy.

This is yet another example of the need to integrate not only forensic sciences with investigative policing requirements, but also with the judicial processes.

Epilogue by Gregg L. Greer[1]

This is an exciting and welcome addition to the practice and study of Forensic Pathology and its implications on criminal investigations into deaths. With thousands of estimated 'suspicious' deaths year by year, understanding of the processes involved, and role of forensic pathology in these investigations by the wider public has never been more vital. Deaths, especially, controversial ones, whether due to Law Enforcement, or others, must at the very least be thoroughly and impartially investigated.

Forensic pathology, as this book shows, has an important role in this process—it helped to shape investigations. It had to be integrated into wider investigations of crime, and was, but there is a further integration that is necessary. Understandably, nothing terrifies the public to a frenzy more than deaths, especially untimely and unfair ones. Most deaths happen suddenly, unexpectedly, and sometimes, violently.

Families, friends, and communities want and demand answers and even more importantly: justice. So urgent is the call for "Communities Worldwide" to find a specialist who can accurately examine the bodies and determine the cause or manner of death (homicide, suicide, accidental, natural or unknown) with a higher level of precision. In my country we face big problems. Too many have died—and are dying in controversial circumstances—elsewhere too.

Satish Sekar has a proven track record of evaluating major crime-scene evidence, including witness statements, but he adds an important aspect to the debate. Forensic pathology has contributed to miscarriages of

1. Bishop Greer is an emerging leader of the new Civil Rights struggle in the USA. He played an important role in securing belated recognition of the shameful injustice suffered by George Stinney Jnr in South Carolina. Stinney was the youngest person to suffer capital punishment in the USA in the last century—June 16th 1944. He was just 14 years-old, but he was also innocent. Stinney was convicted in just ten minutes. His conviction was vacated seventy years later. Stinney's case was widely seen as a great injustice from the past that was important to put right.

   Greer has taken up current cases too. He is a public speaker, Minister, journalist, author, and outstanding social activist. He founded **Freedom First International**. He is a prominent member of the **Southern Christian Leadership Conference** (SCLC). Recently, he became a member of the **United Nations Committee for the Elimination of Racism, Afrophobia and Colorism (UNCERAC)**. He has written for the **Huffington Post**.

justice. It has been happening for decades. Sekar demonstrates that serious injustice has occurred many times, but the case studies are interesting. It is illuminating to discover that it happens in so many jurisdictions. Clearly, progress is essential — some of the changes that were needed are beginning to happen, but the pace of change is slower than I'd like — than our communities need.

I definitely give a strong recommendation to this book — learn it, read it, and add it to your collection!

Abbreviations

ACPO—The Association of Chief Police Officers
ACPOS—The Association of Chief Police Officers of Scotland
ANC—The African National Congress
APLA—The Azanian People's Liberation Army
BBC—The British Broadcasting Corporation
CCRC—The Criminal Cases Review Commission
CCTV—Closed Circuit Television
CID—Criminal Investigation Department
CPS—The Crown Prosecution Service
CSI—Crime Scene Investigator
DNA—Deoxyribonucleic Acid
EDNAP—The European DNA Profiling group
FSR—The Forensic Science Regulator
FSS—The Forensic Science Service
GMC—The General Medical Council
HMCPSI—Her Majesty's Crown Prosecution Service Inspectorate
Hp—Haptoglobin (a blood group)
ILAC—International Laboratory Accreditation Corporation
IPCC—The Independent Police Complaints Commission
IQ—Intelligence Quotient
ISO—International Standards Organisation
JAW—The reference numbers of samples taken by Dr John Whiteside
KC—King's Counsel
LCN—Low Copy Number
NAO—The National Audit Office
NCA—The National Crime Agency
NCF—The National Crime Faculty
NCOF—The National Crime and Operations Faculty
NCP—The National College of Policing
NCPE—The National Centre for Policing Excellence

NPIA—The National Policing Improvement Agency
PAC—The Pan-Africanist Congress of Azania
PACE—The Police And Criminal Evidence Act
PCA—The Police Complaints Authority
PCB—The Police Complaints Board
QC—Queen's Counsel (a top barrister referred to as a 'silk')
RH—The reference numbers of samples taken by Reginald Hearse (a police officer)
SC—Senior Counsel
SGM+—Second Generation Multiplex+[1]
SIO—The Senior Investigating Officer
SOCA—The Serious Organised Crime Agency
SOCO—Scene of Crime Officer
TPU—Timer Power Units
TRC—The Truth and Reconciliation Commission
TWOC—Taking Without the Owner's Consent
UK—United Kingdom
UKAS—United Kingdom Accreditation Service
USA—The United States of America

1. It is called SGM+ because it added four more genes and the gender determination Y-chromosome test to the previous system which had tested at just six genes or loci.

APPENDIX ONE

Interpretation or Manipulation

The Bane

The Lynette White Inquiry is far from the only case to be plagued by misinterpretation of a crime-scene and the failure to integrate the various scientific and investigative disciplines. Some of the problems that have blighted investigations stem from the era of pre-eminence of forensic pathologists—the era of Spilsburyism. Although Sir Bernard's prime was the best part of a century ago, the problems that he and his mentor Sir William Wilcox unleashed, dominated both forensic pathology and investigative policing for several decades. It also led to problems in expert testimony too.

Both Spilsbury and Wilcox were unable to tolerate dissent from their opinions, however well-founded or correct that dissent proved to be, even if it came from eminent experts such as Regius Professor and forensic pathologist Sir Sydney Smith. And, as for admitting the possibility that they could be wrong, well, perish the thought. The highest concession that would ever pass their lips was the all but meaningless admission: "It is possible". Such expert opinion hardly assisted the jury. The real question was 'Is it likely?' rather than 'Is it possible?' So in reality the concession offered in evidence by Wilcox and later Spilsbury was little more than a grudging means of countering any potential or actual damage done to their opinion by giving the implied suggestion that while it was possible, it was not likely and could therefore be discounted by the jury. This assisted the prosecuting barristers, but it came at a price. They were not so enamoured of these experts when they were defending. The modern equivalent is the answer "Technically", to the question, "Is it possible"? That answer means, "I cannot rule that out, but there is no evidence to support it, and it is therefore very unlikely".

Spilsburyism survived Sir Bernard and indeed the second generation of forensic pathologists, Donald Teare, Francis Camps and Keith Simpson too. In fact, its consequences lasted into the new millennium. The Lynette White Inquiry was a case in point. There was no doubt what type of murder this was—it was sadistic. It was exceptionally vicious, but what about the sexual elements? Defence solicitor Stuart Hutton was not convinced. Professor Bernard Knight—now retired—was one of the leading forensic pathologists of his generation. Knight said that there were sexual elements to the murder.

Hutton did not accept that at first, but he was wrong. If anything Knight's opinion was an understatement and it resulted in problems that should never have occurred. There was far more than sexual overtones to Lynette's murder — it was clearly a sexually motivated homicide. If that had been understood and acted upon in 1988 and onwards the whole course that the inquiry went down would have been different — very different.

The Ridiculous Circle

On July 4th 2003 Jeffrey Gafoor's guilty plea not only resolved the Lynette White Inquiry, but also vindicated the Cardiff Five, and the irrefutable evidence. Let's be clear first — the crime-scene, forensic pathology, psychological forensic pathology, blood distribution pattern, especially the cast-off blood pattern, all had a story to tell. And that was a narrative these methods told in unison. It was actually a very simple story — one that even Dr John Whiteside, the architect of the wretched cocktail-hypothesis — believed in for nine months. Whiteside's investigations found not a scrap of scientific evidence that ever supported the hypothesis he later advanced. Whiteside followed where the evidence led — he plainly believed what the evidence was telling him, that it was consistent with one man acting on his own. He even said that man was white — such crimes tended to have been committed by Caucasians or Asians — until he had the misfortune to discover new evidence; a chance blood grouping match to an associate of Lynette. In fact, that 'evidence' was simply a coincidence. It was not even 'one hell of a coincidence' as Whiteside later claimed. It should never have had the impact that it did.

Whiteside never eliminated his initial case-scenario — the one that was supported by evidence — that Lynette's murder was consistent with only one person murdering Lynette, and that the person who did so was a man. Unfortunately, the integrated approach that Professor Barclay, the now retired forensic scientist and Emeritus Professor, favours was not mandatory in 1988 and DNA testing was far from being able to make the telling contribution that it would fifteen years later. Forensic pathology too had not yet broken free of the consequences of Spilsburyism only this time the forensic pathology was not the dominant science — it had a part to play, but its contribution was not told clearly enough. While it may well have been clear to Professor Bernard Knight and others such as forensic scientists and investigators what type of murder this was and what the significance of that was, it was not to the jury, and there was plenty more to mislead them both in 1989, 1990 and again in 2003, 2008 and 2011. For good measure there was a repeat dose in 2016 and that doesn't take the old style committal hearings of February 1989 or the appeals in 1992 into account either. An astonishing eight court hearings occurred without one of them hearing this vital evidence.

Barclay's review established that Whiteside's initial opinion was correct. There was no credible evidence whatsoever that indicated more than one killer. There was plenty that clearly stated the opposite. Lynette was murdered late at night. It was pitch black in the room. The attack occurred in a small part of the room. According to the police and Crown, at least five killers took part and at least two 'coerced' witnesses were involved as well. Of course Lynette was there too, making a total of eight persons apparently charging around in an unlit room. Whiteside had identified what the blood distribution pattern was saying. He correctly identified what was cast-off blood—highly significant as that was the murderer's blood—as opposed to blood-spatter. There was plenty of cast-off blood, but from only one source. This was significant too. It could and should have destroyed the nonsense that was allowed to muddy the waters later (see below) and there was the other highly significant evidence that rubbished the multiple killer hypothesis. There was no evidence supporting it—not a scrap of scientific evidence in circumstances where there should have been plenty of it if it had happened. Not a single drop of blood had been deposited there by any of the Cardiff Five or witnesses. Not a single footwear mark in blood was there tying any of them to the room or victim. There was nothing at all to tie any of the Cardiff Five or alleged eyewitnesses to the room or victim in circumstances that made no sense whatsoever if they had been involved. This evidence was available for all of the 30 years that have passed, yet never has a court heard it and no media has ever mentioned it. None of the reviews have ever considered this damning negative evidence—evidence that proved the innocence of the Cardiff Five and supported the case of Vilday et al from a very early stage. Where is the review of that?

Instead, it took just one day to trump the forensic science—literally—the day Whiteside discovered Angela Psaila's combination of blood groups. Psaila had been brutally raped in early December 1988. That event, totally unrelated to Lynette's murder, turned out to be a pivotal one to the inquiry. It contributed to two of the worst miscarriages of justice to blight British justice, those of the Cardiff Five and the New Cardiff Three (Grommek, Psaila and Vilday). Psaila had the rotten luck to possess exactly the same combination of blood groups as Lynette's murderer, Jeffrey Gafoor, but that should not have mattered. Soon, further tests showed Psaila did not possess the male Y-chromosome and her DNA was of course also different. She should have been eliminated, but Whiteside was convinced that her blood groups had to be relevant—to him she simply had to be involved, but she wasn't and Whiteside should have known that, as it contradicted what the scene assessment said — evidence that had informed his own opinion previously.

If this case, with the same facts, had happened today, the inquiry would not have followed the same discredited course. DNA testing would have categorically eliminated Psaila once and for all, as it did in the reopened investigation of 1999–2003, and with her elimination the case against the Cardiff Five would have been demolished once and for all, as DNA testing established that not a single trace of their DNA was found at the crime-scene. But it should never have come to this even in the 1980s. Tempting as it may be to give the benefit of the doubt to original investigators — DNA testing was not sophisticated enough in 1988–1990 — there are compelling reasons why that should not be done.

The methods used by the retired Head of Physical Evidence at the National Crime Faculty, Professor Dave Barclay in 1999, were available to Dr Whiteside in 1988. In fact, to a lesser degree, they were used by him to establish where to look for the murderer's blood in a crime-scene heavily stained with Lynette's blood. Interestingly, Whiteside discovered cast-off blood that had been shed by the murderer just as he originally suspected. Barclay discovered even more. That built a compelling picture — one that should have ensured that further insult to sound sense and reason was no longer possible. There were reasons Gafoor pleaded guilty in 2003 — most notably the sheer impossibility of any other credible explanation for more than ten different areas of cast-off blood in the murder room, and there was more.

As Gafoor left the scene contact stains were observed too, and Barclay and Angela Gallup independently recommended other areas to test, including under paint inside the front door of 7 James Street. It was among blood that had been preserved by paint for over a decade. There were other contact stains on wallpaper that were never tested, but had been stored for years — the force deserve credit for retaining them. The vital ones included an area of skirting board, where both Barclay and Gallup noticed a drop of cast-off blood on the wall. They both concluded that it would have dripped down the wall to where the skirting board met the wall, remaining in the crevice between wall plaster and wood. That blood could not have been planted for obvious reasons. The skirting board was removed, revealing the blood, which was DNA tested.

It matched the other profiles that had been shed by the killer. It was Gafoor's DNA on the wall, under the paint on the door, on the wallpaper and on cellophane found on the bed. Faced with this plethora of incontrovertible evidence, Gafoor bowed to the inevitable—his guilt had been proved. On July 4th 2003 he accepted that and pleaded guilty. He never resiled from that despite the best efforts of lawyers determined to portray the Cardiff Five guilty despite the clear picture that the indisputable evidence had given.

Scientifically Ludicrous

The suggestion that five men committed what was then the most brutal murder of its type in Welsh history was at best preposterous, but it was even worse. The space was limited. It was dark. They were alleged to have committed a brutal sexually motivated homicide, but decided to leave two other sex-workers alive and well as witnesses against them. They were alleged to have achieved all this and more without leaving any trace of themselves in the flat or on the victim, or had any trace of her on them either. It stretched credibility to absurd lengths.

Professor Barclay demolished that scenario. "The curious thing about John Whiteside's case was that for eight or nine months he was working under the basis that it was a single male that had stabbed Lynette White, that that male had cut himself during the act and had spread blood at the scene", Barclay explains. "Remember there's no DNA, or DNA's just coming in. He identified the blood on the wall as cast-off, exactly the same as Angela Gallup did and exactly the same as I did. That's why that blood was targeted in particular. He also identified that since the body had been dragged, blood on the socks and the bottom of the trousers might well be that of the offender—a mixture of course of offender blood and Lynette White's blood".

That was all correctly based on where the evidence was leading Dr Whiteside, and interestingly the mixture of Lynette's blood and her killer's on her jeans, was the only evidence-based cocktail of blood in this case. But then it went off the rails. "Suddenly, he changed his mind about that and he changed his mind about that because he discovered that the blood groups from Angela Psaila, who was a person associated with Lynette White, were exactly the same as the blood groups that he got from the wall at the scene and those blood groups were 1:3800 or 1:7600 depending on whether you take into account that it's male blood, so let's say it's one in 3800", Barclay said. "He jumped to the conclusion that that blood had come from Angela Psaila".

But how valid was that 'conclusion' and was it even significant?

"Well, it's significant if you look at it from the wrong way round", Barclay said. "If you think Angela Psaila is one of three or four friends of this girl. Her blood is at the scene—blood matching her at the scene—well that cannot be coincidence. Of course it could be coincidence and it actually was coincidence, because the real test of significance is how likely is the blood to get there from any other person in Cardiff, not from one or two of her friends. Not only that, but it didn't actually match her because we now know that it contained male material and DNA that was completely different, but from a blood grouping point of view, he regarded it as being such a coincidence that it could not be a coincidence".

But it didn't add up even in terms of techniques available at that time. "Dr Gill thought that test [his test that was extremely sensitive for the male Y-chromosome] indicated that it was male blood", Barclay said. "Immediately the link was drawn between the blood at the scene and Angela Psaila, other matters started to come up which indicated that it probably wasn't. There were a number of different things that didn't quite fit. For a start, for eight or nine months John Whiteside had been labouring under the misapprehension, as he now thought, that this was a single male. There was no evidence of any other person that was in the flat and that this person had cut himself on the knife which is a very common thing to do in repeated stabbings. Now, it becomes blood from a girl. Well why would the girl have cut herself? Why would the girl be bleeding at the scene in any case?"

These were all valid questions. Why had they not been asked when it might have made a difference?

"He had to explain away the distribution of the blood — perfectly correct if somebody's hand is flying about in the air casting off blood, but not at all consistent with a girl who as far as he knows has not got any bleeding place on her", Barclay explained. "The police then manage to produce for him evidence that Angela Psaila had been bleeding from the mouth and at that point John Whiteside had another difficulty because there is no saliva test from that blood on the wall, though maybe it's gone off, or there isn't any. It's not in a position — there's no flecks on the floor of blood and saliva, which you would expect if somebody is bleeding from the mouth".

It simply did not add up and that should have been obvious to Whiteside and also to the peer-reviewer, or would have been if Whiteside's work had been peer-reviewed as it plainly should have been.

"The pattern is completely wrong" Barclay continued. "There isn't drops on the way out. Drops are on the wall where it would be cast-off from the hand and, crucial point, Lynette White has bled out on the floor. There are no footwear marks in blood from as it turned out, eight or nine people who must have been charging about in a darkened room. Really that is *ludicrously* improbable. John Whiteside would never have thought of that scenario in the first place. I mean people would have laughed at him had he said right from the start without the evidence of Angela Psaila's blood, 'I think it's eight or nine people have done this and they've been charging around here stabbing her and stuff like that'. *Nonsense*" [his emphasis].

It beggars belief that all this and more was not exposed earlier when it could and should have prevented one of Britain's most notorious miscarriages of justice from happening.

Pathological

The blood distribution and crime-scene evidence ought to have demolished the Crown's case back in 1989. The evidence that Barclay used to explain why it was nonsense was available to Whiteside and indeed he used it for eight months, but there is far more. The forensic pathology also had a story to tell and it too was very clear, or rather it ought to have been. Lynette was murdered in 1988, long before forensic pathology was brought into line with the requirements of modern investigation of homicides. There were dire consequences of that.

Professor Bernard Knight was at that time one of the most eminent forensic pathologists practising in Britain. In the early hours of February 15th he conducted the post-mortem examination of Lynette's body. He described and numbered wounds that had been inflicted. According to Knight the first offensive wounds were the triangular cuts to her throat—most blood was lost from them. He would qualify that opinion a bit when he gave evidence in 2011, but he did not change it. He did, however, explain why he thought it. This would pose problems later as lawyers tried to absurdly square the circle by stating boldly that there had been two attacks in order to contest the obvious innocence of the Cardiff Five (see below). Another issue to emerge was that such murders are frenzied and in the course of committing them the killer—I use the singular because such crimes usually are committed by killers acting on their own and because that is what the evidence pointed to in this case—is likely to hit bone. That and the fact that the knife would become slippery with blood means that it is likely that the killer's hand would slip down the handle onto the blade. Consequently, he would cut himself and would cast-off blood. The blood distribution pattern would indicate that. It is what happened in this case. They would have searched for that for these reasons and did. As Barclay points out only one person's cast-off blood was discovered in the flat—all Gafoor's. But how could that have happened if there were five killers and they inflicted the most serious wounds?

The other major issue to emerge from the pathology was the location of most of the wounds. Lynette was not raped, nor was she sexually assaulted, but she was undoubtedly the victim of a sexually motivated homicide. Why?

At least twenty-five of the fifty wounds were to her breasts or chest area—another three, or even four were close by. It is therefore obvious that the killer successfully targeted her breasts, even through her Puffa jacket. In other words, he attacked her femininity. Gregory Bull QC, representing Thomas Page, pointed out that Gafoor was even asked during his interviews with police if he had a fetish with Lynette's breasts, which indicates that those lawyers were aware that this was a sexually motivated homicide, but even though Bull had opened the door the prosecution team made no effort to exploit it. The term 'sexually motivated homicide' was not used in 1988, but there was no doubt what this was. Professor Knight's woolly expression that there were 'sexual overtones' to the murder in no way explained the characteristics of this murder, or the murderer. Understanding this would have affected both the investigation and trials that followed.

Any competent psychological profiler, as they used to be called, would be clear about the significance. They couldn't have predicted important things about Gafoor because he was a very unusual killer—he didn't follow the usual pattern of building up to such violence or continuing after the blood-lust had been awakened—but there were things that could be predicted. There is not one example in all the annals of crime anywhere in the world where five men took it in turns to stab a young woman in a sexually motivated homicide and allowed two other young sex workers to remain alive after making a couple of cuts—the idea being to make them accomplices and therefore unable to testify. It implied that they knew the complexities of law and fails to account for the obvious. Why would five men commit one particularly vicious sexually motivated homicide and not three, especially as that would have eliminated the witnesses to their crime? And even more importantly, there is not a scrap of credible evidence tying these five men and at least two alleged eyewitnesses to presence in that room when Lynette was the victim of that sexually motivated homicide, while there is plenty tying Gafoor alone to his crime.

The Corridor of Uncertainty

Our criminal justice system is adversarial rather than inquisitorial. It is inevitable that trials would be adversarial. But there is a price to pay for this and it's a huge one. Despite the wishes of the former Lord Chief Justice Baron (John) Thomas of Cwmgiedd, expressed while a Lord Justice of Appeal, that experts discuss their findings in advance, that didn't happen in this case and understandably so. Gafoor's conviction began an investigation of what had gone wrong in the original investigation. Unfortunately, the desire to avenge trumped the will to inform. Thirty-four people were arrested and interviewed under caution under suspicion of having committed various offences, including perjury during the inquiry. Twenty of them had been police officers. Three core *civilian* witnesses were jailed for eighteen months. Later, in 2011 eight former officers and two civilian witnesses stood trial. Five other former officers were facing trial later. The trial collapsed in December 2011, but not before it had become clear how inept the prosecution had been.[1]

The forensic pathology was clear, or rather it ought to have been, but the strategy of the defence lawyers in 2011 became clear very quickly. They trod the discredited path of insisting that the Cardiff Five had not suffered a miscarriage of justice at all and that they were in fact guilty. They were allowed to do this in spite of the evidence pointing clearly to the opposite conclusion. It was impossible to suggest that Gafoor had no involvement at all in Lynette's murder—the DNA and the man himself made it clear that he was. Gafoor insisted that he alone was responsible. Incredibly, they refused to accept it and tried to make out that he was in fact innocent and that the Cardiff Five were guilty after all. They latched on to an inconsistent account that Gafoor had given to his QC, John Charles Rees, and his claim that he only remembered inflicting ten or twelve wounds and not the crucial throat wounds. Gafoor insisted that regardless of his poor memory—it may well have been a very convenient one too—he did not associate with any of the Cardiff Five and had not committed the murder with them or anyone else for that matter. Gafoor tried to take ownership of his crime, but defence lawyers William Coker QC, Malcolm Bishop QC, Gregory Bull, and others would not allow it. His memory of inflicting only twelve wounds apparently indicated another attack had taken place and that allowed them to suggest that the Cardiff Five were still guilty regardless of their acquittal or convictions quashed on appeal or Gafoor's guilty plea and conviction. So was it likely, or even probable that there had been more than one attack on the unfortunate Lynette?

Not according to Professor Barclay. "With how many stab wounds?" Barclay asks while laughing with incredulity at the suggestion. "Jeffrey [Gafoor] just did one? Well you can poop that straight away. You can see that of the stab wounds all but a very few

1. Rather than rehearse those facts here I will deal only with the forensic pathology issues here. For further information on a scandalous attempt to reconvict the Cardiff Five see **Trials and Tribulations—Innocence Matters?** which was published in 2017.

are on the breasts, but she's had her neck cut as well and wrists and so on. There's a slash across the face. It's a sexually motivated homicide — full stop. No there cannot be [any doubt about that] and I use it in my lectures to forensic psychology students and as soon as I say, what sort of murder is this and as soon as I show the picture without the puffa jacket it's a sexually motivated homicide and don't forget those stab wounds are through the puffa jacket and clothing and yet they're still, they're all concentrated on the breasts. *It's a single male sexually motivated homicide.* It's a sexually motivated homicide. He's completely lost it, but the grouping [of wounds] is so good that he is targeting stabbing the breasts even through the puffa jacket".

This is damning, or ought to have been. There never was a scrap of evidence that any of the Cardiff Five had any motivation or inclination to commit a sexually motivated homicide. There was no evidence whatsoever that there were two attacks and there was no explanation of how it was possible that Gafoor could have inflicted comparatively minor injuries with cast-off blood in several areas and the others inflicted the far more serious injuries without having cut themselves or left cast-off blood anywhere or leaving footwear marks in blood. But despite being available to give this evidence — evidence that would have undermined these claims, Barclay was not called as a witness, even after the defence tactics became obvious.

So what would Barclay have said if he had been called?

"I would have said where's the evidence for any of that bullshit?" Barclay said. "I might even have said that in court. I would have said all the stuff about the Lynette scene I just said to you now, if I had been called in that trial. It is ludicrous in the extreme and their story is even more ludicrous than John Whiteside's version, w*hich has been scientifically disproved of course*" [his emphasis].

The Modern Spilsburyism

Everyone is entitled to a defence, but this one had consequences. Innocent lives had been wrecked. For the best part of a decade and a half the Cardiff Five had suffered an unjustified whispering campaign. They had been branded murderers despite the lack of credible evidence and once the accusation had been made it stuck. The criminal justice system does not make findings of innocence. A not guilty verdict includes the innocent, but legally it is no more than a finding that the defendant has not been proven guilty beyond reasonable doubt. The same applies on appeal. A quashed conviction includes the innocent, but it is no more than a finding that the conviction was not safe. Neither is a declaration of innocence. So despite the absurdity of the case against them the

Cardiff Five remained in legal limbo — their innocence obvious to all but those who refuse to see, but with no official acknowledgement of it. All that changed on July 4th 2003 when Gafoor's conviction vindicated them. But it would not last.

The officers accused of framing the Cardiff Five refused to accept that they had done anything wrong and mounted an outrageous defence. Despite the lack of credible evidence against the Cardiff Five and the overwhelming evidence that Gafoor was guilty of Lynette's murder and had committed the crime on his own, they insisted that they had not been wrong and that the Cardiff Five had been guilty. The evidence against Gafoor could not be totally ignored — it was obvious that he was involved, but they were determined to square the circle. The tactic became clear early — the cross-examinations of Gafoor began by trying to link him to the Cardiff Five. There was no link and Gafoor tried to take responsibility, but that was not what they wanted to hear. They all but suggested that a man who pleaded guilty due to overwhelming evidence was not really guilty after all. The clear implication was that he had not inflicted the first offensive wounds. If that was true then Gafoor did not kill Lynette. It was absurd. How could Gafoor have cut himself if he only inflicted minor wounds? How had his blood been cast-off on the wall? What was he doing and how was the pattern consistent with cast-off blood during a vicious attack if he was not actually stabbing her repeatedly? And of course there was no evidence at all that was consistent with a second attack. If Gafoor had gone first and inflicted only minor wounds, when had he left? Why had Lynette not raised the alarm after the first attack? Exactly which wounds do they claim Gafoor inflicted? This scenario defied logic on so many levels. Nevertheless, this was their defence and they were sticking to it.

According to some the consultant forensic scientist Angela Gallup supported the two attacks hypothesis. She did nothing of the sort. The closest that she came to anything approaching that came in the following exchange with William Coker QC on behalf of Graham Mouncher. "[I]f he's right about stabbing her, making ten or twelve stabbing gestures, obviously then there's more to it than that, but let's suppose — and it is suppose obviously — but let's suppose there is a Gafoor struggle which leaves the blood on the outer wall and so on, and he leaves, depositing his blood as he goes", Coker said. "Then the fatal attack could come minutes or even hours later, couldn't it, involving someone completely different?"

"Well, technically, if Lynette White didn't bleed and if the stab cuts, you know, in her clothing accord with what he has described, so, you know, it all looks like it fits together, then that — I mean, I couldn't comment about that" Gallop replied. "I mean, that's — you know, it's possible".

But the clothing did not accord with him having inflicted ten or twelve stab wounds. This was the crux of the defence case. If Gafoor had inflicted all of the wounds as he repeatedly told the court in 2011, there was only one attack. He also made it very clear that nobody else was responsible. Gallop's response was far from an endorsement of the defence scenario that there had been two attacks. It was, at most, an acknowledgement that the possibility could not be ruled out, but was it likely? Not according to Professor Barclay. "Okay, I probably couldn't rule out the possibility, but I can say, 'taking into account it's a sexually motivated homicide and the pattern of it, it's so unlikely as to be in practical terms impossible', but that's a matter for the jury to decide", Barclay said.

He was available to give evidence, but was never called, even after it became clear what the defence tactics were and that scientifically ludicrous scenarios were being advanced without being challenged, or at least as effectively as they could have been. Barclay demolishes the scenario. "You could have got a forensic psychologist to say the same", he said. "Okay, somebody commits a murder that's really unlucky for Lynette White and then he goes away. She's got loads of wounds that are fatal, or would be fatal within ten minutes or something like that. In that ten minute period, somebody else comes and she's allegedly still alive and stabs her another thirty times — a group. Has that ever happened before in the UK from a forensic psychologist's point of view? No, so therefore that's Occam's Razor. It's actually very, very, very unlikely, isn't it? Never mind about how many people, or anything else, just the fact one person stabs somebody and somebody else comes along by chance and chooses to stab them again, now in a sexually motivated way? No, it has never happened as far as I am aware".

So it was clear. The forensic pathology, the psychological pathology, the offender psychology, the blood distribution pattern, the crime-scene analysis and more besides had told and continued to tell a clear and concise story. Lynette White was the victim of a sexually motivated homicide. All the crime-scene and scientific evidence, when integrated with each other, showed it had been committed by one killer acting on his own and that man as he freely and repeatedly admitted was Jeffrey Gafoor. Given so clear a picture, based on such strong evidence, it beggars belief that the Cardiff Five were not only accused of the murder again in 2011, but also in the 2015 proceedings where several officers tried to get compensated over the Phase III investigation. Those proceedings once again ignored the evidence referred to above which proved the innocence of the Cardiff Five.

APPENDIX 2

Dr Charles Smith — the Canadian Spilsbury

Controversy and Case Studies

Dr Charles Smith had been appointed as the head of paediatric forensic pathology in Ontario. He had not been trained in forensic pathology, yet had a 30-year career in that capacity. During the 1990s his reputation and influence grew, along with growing doubts about the quality of his work. In 2005 an independent and international review team looked at 44 of his cases. It concluded that 20 of those cases were problematic. In 2007, Justice Stephen Goudge of the Court of Appeal for Ontario was appointed to head up an inquiry into his work. The findings of the inquiry revealed some appalling cases.

Amber, aged 16 months, 1988: Dr Smith said that there was 'no possibility what-so-ever' that Amber's injuries had resulted from a fall down a few carpeted stairs as the baby-sitter had claimed. He said you would have to drop the child from three storeys to kill her like that. After the trial, the baby-sitter was acquitted of manslaughter. The judge said that Smith did not understand the science of 'shaken-baby' syndrome, had failed to keep proper records, to make proper inquiries and lacked objectivity. Justice Goudge also found Smith had made false and misleading statements.

Nicholas, aged 11 months, 1995: the mother said the child had died after falling from a standing position. Dr Smith said he was '99 per cent certain' that the boy had died from non-accidental injuries. Proceedings were undertaken over ward-ship of the child the mother was expecting. An independent specialist said that Smith's findings went 'well beyond the forensic and scientific facts'. Justice Goudge found that a report by the deputy chief coroner at the time had misled people into thinking that Smith had been correct. Further proceedings against the coroner were dropped after he gave an undertaking never to practice medicine again.

Jenna, aged under two years, 1997: the baby died after being left in the care of a 14-year-old boy. Dr Smith said she had died from injuries sustained some 24 hours before she died. The mother was charged with her murder. Subsequently, Smith agreed the injuries must have occurred whilst in the care of the babysitter. Unexamined evidence relating to the case was later found in Smith's office. Justice Goudge again found that Smith had made false or misleading statements.

Sharon, aged 7 years, 1997: She was found dead in the basement of her home with dozens of penetrating wounds to her body. Dr Smith concluded she had died from multiple stab wounds. He said it would be as absurd to think that a polar bear had attacked her as it would be to suggest they were injuries caused by a dog. After an independent inquiry, murder charges against the mother were withdrawn after it was found that the injuries were in fact dog bite-marks. Justice Goudge said that Smith's errors were 'basic' and the results had been 'catastrophic'.

Valin, aged 4 years, 1993: Dr Smith said the young girl had been sexually assaulted and had died from asphyxiation. She had been in the care of her uncle Bill Mullins-Johnson. After being convicted of murder, he spent 12 years in jail before it was established that Valin had not been sexually assaulted or murdered. The uncle said he had to live every day with the thought that he was about to be killed — because that's what they do to people like him in prison. Justice Goudge found that Smith's opinions were speculative and unsubstantiated and that he often responded to criticism in ways that were 'unprofessional, arrogant and unjustified'.

Legal Procedures

The Goudge Report had much sound advice about how to improve forensic services and the government of Ontario has since invested one billion dollars to establish a forensic science centre in Toronto which is the envy of the world.

Where wrongful convictions have occurred in Canada, they occasionally establish a judicial inquiry to investigate the causes of the wrongful conviction. Being set up after the conviction has been overturned, the experts called to the Commission will know that their work has already been subjected to scrutiny in the appeal process. The standard procedure of the inquiry is to conduct an international comparative review of the issues arising in the case to see how other jurisdictions have responded to similar problems. The reports of the eight inquiries to date are an invaluable source of information about defective investigative and prosecutorial practices.

It should be noted that at least six of the judicial inquiries have recommended the establishment of a Criminal Cases Review Commission, although those recommendations have not been acted upon to date.

Whilst the Canadian appeal procedures are similar to those of the UK, the most notable differences arise in the area of the petition applications for wrongful conviction cases. Petitions are directed to the federal attorney-general, not the state attorney-general. The federal attorney-general has powers which have not been available in the

UK or Australia. The attorney can set the conviction aside and order a new trial, or refer the matter directly to the Supreme Court in addition to the more usual power of referral to the court of appeal. In addition, in considering a petition, the attorney has guidelines which are publicly available. After the initial review, the attorney will release to the parties draft reasons for a pending decision, which will enable them to provide feedback. Final reasons for the subsequent decision are also made available.

The Motherisk Program

This hair-strand testing process was used to establish the presence of drugs and alcohol. The results were used to convict people of criminal offences or to establish that parents were unfit to care for their children. Concerns have been raised that preliminary screening tests were being used instead of proper confirmatory tests. The program was suspended in March 2015 and various judicial inquiries have been taking place.

Dr Smith's Demise

Meanwhile, Dr Smith's career is over. In 2002 he was reprimanded over his conduct in three suspicious death autopsies by the Ontario College of Physicians and Surgeons and was later suspended from performing autopsies. Prior to that, his position was all but unchallenged—he even trained lawyers on questioning expert witnesses in court and much more besides. After his suspension in 2003, he secured a new post in Saskatchewan, but had failed to disclose that he had been under investigation in Ontario at the time. That cost him that job ultimately. His registration ended in 2008, but in February 2011 he pleaded 'no contest' to charges of 'disgraceful conduct'. He was stripped of his medical licence. As we have seen, his conduct had resulted in many serious miscarriages of justice.

Lightning Source UK Ltd.
Milton Keynes UK
UKHW021414180220
358911UK00004B/223

9 780952 732525